UNDER-
GROUND

Underground
The Subterranean World of DIY Punk Shows

Daniel Makagon

Edited by Taylor Hurley and Joe Biel
Designed by Joe Biel
Cover design by Meggyn Pomerleau
Cover photo courtesy of Beau Patrick, beaupatrickcoulon.com

Interior photos by
Bull Gervasi, pages 4-5, 31, 34, 56, 65, 74, 101, 115, 120, 149, 152
Joseph Gervasi, page 119
John Harmon, endhymns.com, pages 97-98, 113
Patrick Houdek, patrickhoudekphotography.com, back cover, pages 46, 86, 102, 111
Craig Kamrath, craigkamrath.tumblr.com, pages 15, 18, 93, 188, 207, 223, inside covers
Dave Zukauskas, rockscissorsgun.tumblr.com, pages 7, 44, 67, 80, 94, 127, 204

Microcosm Publishing
2752 N Williams Ave.
Portland, OR 97227
www.microcosmpublishing.com

ISBN 978-1-62106-518-0
First Published September 15, 2015
First printing of 3,000 copies
Distributed by Legato / Perseus Books Group and Turnaround, U.K.

Printed on post-consumer paper with sustainable inks in the U.S.

UNDER-GROUND

DANIEL MAKAGON

Contents

Section

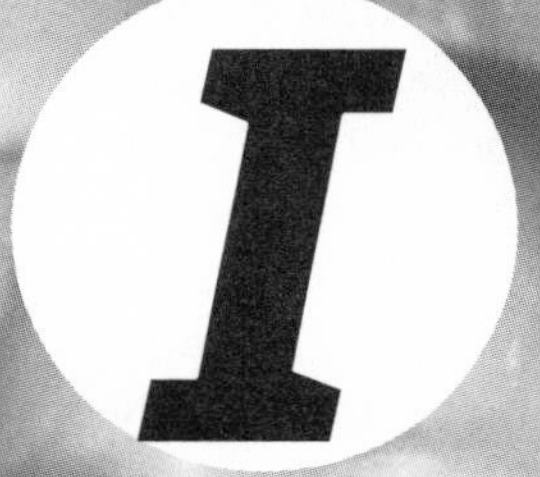

Discovery

Avail crowd, 10/5/94 Fake House, Cabbage Collective Show, West Philadelphia

A few minutes ago there were small pockets of smoke in the basement, but the smoke has been slowly and steadily expanding to fill the space. People would normally be quick to run when faced with a situation like this, knowing the old adage that where there's smoke, there's fire. But nobody is leaving. Everyone here understands that sparklers produced the fire in this instance and smoke followed. By the time the smoke from the burnt-out sparklers had subsided the fog machine was fully functioning, spewing chemically produced fog that is filling the space. It's probably not too wise for the 70 people who are here to inhale these carcinogens for the next 25 minutes, but sometimes celebration and aesthetics override rationality.

We have gathered in the basement of Albion House, one of Chicago's longest-running punk houses, to see four bands. The bill is packed with some of the scene's more active participants, including the return of Miriam Bastani. Miriam left the city a few years back to become a coordinator at *Maximum Rocknroll* (*MRR*) and has returned with her Bay Area band Permanent Ruin. Also on the bill are Weekend Nachos, who have been together for a long time by punk standards and are one of the better-known powerviolence bands in the United States. Tensions, made up of ex-members of some of the city's foundational Latino punk bands, was the first band to play, about 90 minutes ago. Now Cold Lovers is about to start. This is their last show, so they thought it would be fun to hand out the sparklers and to rent the fog machine. The aesthetic features of their set are a lot artier than one would normally encounter during the standard Chicago punk-rock basement show. In addition to the sparklers and fog machine, the band has opted for a make-shift light show that consists of a dim yellow glow emitting from the lone exposed light bulb that is left on and the flickering images of Yanni, or some such New Age musician, on an old standard-definition TV set that sits behind the band. The overall experience builds in intensity during the second-to-last song, "Mouth." This five-minute song, which is lengthy by punk standards, blends the beefiness of some early-to-mid-'90s bands (The Jesus Lizard, Tar, The Cows) with straight-ahead punk rock vocals. The lyrics screamed by Carrie, the band's singer, repeat ("I wanna mouth with you/I've never mouthed before/I wanna put my mouth on you/Let's mouth"), mirroring the repetitive chord changes and rhythm. The song's recurring groove blends with the smoke and flickering video to create a hypnotic mood, which would seem to fit more naturally with a hard psych band than a punk band. But the deviation from the normal do-it-yourself (DIY) punk experience is cool. The crowd, as is the case with almost all punk shows, adds to the vibe. In this instance, the song inspires a slower motion mosh from one side of the graffiticovered basement to the other. As "Mouth" fades out via a wall of feedback, I feel as if I have been dropped into an avant-garde re-enactment of a scene from *Apocalypse Now*, staged in the basement of Albion House instead of a Saigon-inspired location in the Philippines.

There is a lot about this particular show in this specific space that is quite ordinary for participants in the DIY punk scene. The interactions prior to the show, when bands play, time between the sets, and once the show has finished are fairly common. It is the only time I have seen people lighting fireworks in the basement during a show, although there have been some sporadic posts in punk music forums about Chicago punks lighting fireworks in the past. About a year after this show

Ampere at The Whitney House in Hartford, CT 7/1/09

I heard the singer from Denver hardcore band Negative Degree ask a local punk about policies regarding lighting off fireworks. Perhaps a city rebuilt post-Great Fire has an unhealthy obsession with fire built into its collective DNA. Or maybe there is something about the rebellion of punk for some people that leads them to think that the ordinary energy of a DIY punk show is not enough. Dave K. wrote in a June 2006 letter to *MRR* about a similar situation at ABC No Rio in New York City: "At one show, some brain surgeon though[t] it would be fun to start lighting off fireworks in the pit area. Nobody got hurt, but it could have caused some problems."

Of course, gathering in a basement to see four punk bands probably seems like a strange thing to someone outside the DIY scene. Most people's basements are used for storing lawnmowers or snow shovels. These dark, damp, spider-infested spaces are not imagined as sites to hang out unless the basement has been finished, functioning as a playroom for the kids, a spot for teens to escape their parents, or an extra TV room developed to facilitate Dad's sports-fandom escape. Instead, the mainstream music industry's version of live performance seems normal for mainstream music fans: advance ticket sales and progressively increasing set times, as the opening local band gives way to a touring support act who is followed by the headliner. Multiple options usually exist for buying alcohol (cocktail waitresses and waiters, bartenders, more than one bar if the space is larger). And there is often a large merchandise booth where tour memorabilia is sold for high prices. The band plays on a large stage, and lights are carefully choreographed with the music to create an entertainment experience.

Even fans of punk who spend most of their time listening to better-known forms of the music would also likely consider the house show to be an oddity. People who listen to major label manufactured mall punk are unlikely to even know about smaller clubs and bars that host punk concerts. And most fans of bands on independent labels that almost exclusively play bars, clubs, or auditoriums—even bands signed with Fat Wreck Chords, a large and independent punk label—are not generally tuned into the DIY scene even if the bands themselves have played these spaces in the past. Houses are not the only sites where one can find DIY punk shows. Community-based non-profit spaces, VFW halls, art galleries, and record stores also host punk shows. And there is also a range of sporadic, one-off "generator shows" that are organized along riverfronts, in abandoned parking garages, or in the woods. Stable community-based, volunteer-run venues have a better chance of registering with fans of more well-known indie punk bands, but the reality is that most people who listen to punk in the U.S. see bands in bars and clubs; these music fans move through the world mostly unaware that DIY show spaces exist.

The people who are inspired to book DIY shows, the bands that would rather play in these spaces than at a bar or club, and the participants who turn up to see the bands collectively continue a long history of DIY punk. These individual and collective efforts also slightly repurpose and re-frame how punk is lived and shared. DIY shows have historically been infused with a desire to blur the boundaries between performer and audience, to jointly shape the rules that govern live music performances, to model and live an alternative economic system, and to come together in contexts that do not provide profit for organizations and individuals who work outside the DIY scene.

I wanted to examine these spaces in an effort to understand the nuances of different types of DIY music places, how such spaces embody an alternative way of being together, and how the spaces fit into a larger DIY touring network in the U.S. Moreover, I wanted to consider the reasons why DIY spaces and DIY touring matter to punk music and culture in the U.S. The historical and contemporary stories of touring bands and DIY promoters help others inside the scene gain a better understanding of DIY show spaces. Additionally, I hope that the larger narrative of DIY punk shows can inspire people outside the scene to consider an alternative model for cultural production.

• • •

I was introduced to punk by a friend's older brother when I was nine years old. I grew up in Southern California, which was an amazing location for punk at that time. After discovering important bands like The Ramones, Sex Pistols, X-Ray Spex, and Buzzcocks, I started negotiating with my parents for early payment of allowances so I could buy records from the then-local bands, who are now considered the foundation of U.S. punk and hardcore. These bands were putting out their first 7"s, EPs, and albums: Black Flag's *Jealous Again* came out around that time, Circle Jerks released *Group Sex*, and the Germ's *GI* was issued. I was finding out about these bands through word-of-mouth but also listened religiously to Rodney Bingenheimer's weekly show on KROQ FM, *Rodney on the Roq*, which featured a mix of punk, rockabilly, mod, and psych bands. And his first compilation on Posh Boy introduced me to the world of fanzines; it included *Flipside* fanzine number twenty-one. A few years later I would discover Andrea Enthal's radio show on KPFK FM, *12 O'Clock Rock*, which presented a more international vision of punk. And I found a textual complement to *12 O'Clock Rock* in *MRR*. Southern California-based chain record stores like Music Plus and Licorice Pizza carried a variety of punk records and sold some fanzines. And independent record stores were selling domestic releases and imports.

Fanzines and the liner notes in these records became resources to learn about bands and the unique features of different local scenes. Moreover, the flyers for shows, again found at both local chains and independent shops, helped flesh out a punk rock aesthetic while modeling an alternative to big budgets for advertising and public relations, and music marketing. My first discovery of punk set in motion the belief that punk can have a powerful influence on how we live and live together.

As I got older, I learned that I was not alone. Other kids my age had been finding out about punk at that same time. Although we thought we were alone in the musical landscape, discovering a genre of music that was radically at odds with bands like Queen, Styx, and Fleetwood Mac that ruled commercial radio and adorned the T-shirts of our friends, most of us would quickly learn that there were other people in cities and towns near and far who were feeling the same energy and finding the same inspiration in punk. Discovery of punk may not have been uniform, but scenes were developing organically and quickly throughout the U.S.

Fanzines, college radio, local access cable video shows, and flyers continue to introduce people to the art and politics of punk rock. And these older media now exist alongside blogs, websites, music streaming, downloading options, and other social media. New media resources simultaneously help us learn about the most niche cultural forms and flatten out our experiences by compressing time and space so that anyone anywhere can now hear the most obscure old and new punk bands. We can see YouTube videos that teach us how to dance and how to stand, what T-shirts we should wear, and the slang that we should adopt. And there are now a range of corporate chain stores that will sell us punk-rock identity kits in the form of outfits, posters, and records. However, that process of finding punk and instantly feeling energized continues to play out for young kids, teenagers, and those who are older. You can find these expressions of passionate discovery in the letters section of fanzines, posted on message boards, added to comments columns on blogs, and sometimes in the manic conversation between a new fan and a record store owner. There remains something unique, often inviting, about punk media that helps listeners, readers, and viewers develop some sense of what it means to be punk. Amidst the ironic and sometimes snotty discourse one regularly finds passionate messages that you should be doing this too: writing, making art, or starting a band. But that media takes us only so far. There is a shift that occurs when we move from consuming punk media to attending a punk show. The punk show helps us discover what it feels like to *do* punk. As Adriana from Hysterics notes in a February 2015 *MRR* interview with Viktor Vargyai, there can be a disconnection between punk's cultural politics and one's everyday life (especially for teenagers first discovering the music). "Through a process of going to shows and showing up and interacting with people, getting involved in different projects, it became more of a visceral experience," Adriana says.

As a little kid I wasn't attending punk shows even though the local bands and the second wave of British punk (UK82) touring bands were playing large all-ages venues, such as Olympic Auditorium, Fenders Ballroom, and Santa Monica Civic Center. (See the numerous *Flipside* video comps from that time for footage of these venues.) But a step below these large spaces was the club and bar scene, which meant a 21-year-old age limit. Los Angeles has historically been poor when it comes to all-ages options, although some of that changed in the early '90s and continues to get better with various houses doing shows and DIY record stores hosting bands. By the time I was in college at Loyola Marymount University and DJing/working as the Music Director at KXLU FM, a variety of all-ages DIY spaces appeared. Most notably, Jabberjaw featured DIY bands that fit into the punk genre broadly speaking. Additionally, straight edge hardcore shows were happening somewhat regularly at warehouses in Orange County (although larger touring bands tended to play so-called legitimate medium-sized venues, such as the Country Club in Reseda). When I finished college, I moved to New York City, where the bulk of my time was spent in bars and clubs. Most clubs were booking indie rock and alternative rock bands. CBGB, one of the most iconic punk clubs, was no longer doing hardcore matinees and rarely hosted shows that featured bands involved with the DIY punk scene. Wetlands, a club in TriBeCa, was doing some punk matinees. Garage and garage-punk bands were playing at The Continental, but this was also a bar. ABC No Rio was *the* DIY option for hardcore shows and the only full-time all-ages option.

It wasn't until I moved to Chicago in 2005 that I really experienced a DIY scene that was, and is still, healthy enough to provide a true alternative to clubs and bars. Of course, house, basement, and other DIY shows existed in many cities between the time I left New York in 1993 and my move to Chicago, but the cities in which I lived during that window were limited when it came to DIY spaces (a return to Los Angeles, then to Tampa, and the rural Upper Peninsula of Michigan). In part, the difference between Los Angeles and New York in the early 1990s and various cities throughout the U.S. now when it comes to DIY show spaces is a product of a changing alternative musical landscape for shows. But the distinctions between these time periods are also informed by what people are willing to do in their cities. LA and New York are both better now for DIY show options, but both pale in comparison to some smaller cities, which on the surface would seem odd given the size of the populations in LA and New York, and the variety of complementary punk media (again, zines, college radio, and even other Bohemian cultural activities). Perhaps the quantity of options in a larger city functions as a mirage. People feel as if they have everything they need when it comes to alternative forms of music: radio, record stores, multiple clubs. But these cities lack steady DIY spaces.

Ultimately, my move to Chicago in 2005 was transformative and inspirational because I could regularly attend house shows, which I started to do a year or so later. The house shows taught me something new about a genre of music and a cultural identity that has been a central feature of my life for a long, long time. In this respect, *Underground* emerges from a mix of my converging interests, which include a long-term connection to punk and a consistent research focus on space and place, community and public life, and DIY culture since I started graduate studies in communication in 1995.

I have never been in a band, nor have I booked a show. And although I had interviewed bands on the radio and talked with them about touring, most of those conversations were part of the regular Q&A conventions of broadcast interviews. (Fanzine interviews tend to mirror radio interviews but usually include a lot more profanity.) Questions about shows and touring are part of a larger list of mostly standardized questions about songs (both meanings and recording processes), about band formation, about working with labels, about other favorite bands and influences, maybe socio-political topics of the day, and then some fairly forgettable banter.

In the past ten years there has been a rapid proliferation of books and documentaries about punk music and culture that have gone deeper than the average radio interview or fanzine feature. Collectively, these texts and films fill in historical gaps while foregrounding previously obscure features of punk music and culture. Most tend to focus on a particular punk scene or city, such as the documentary, *You Weren't There: A History of Chicago Punk, 1977-1984* or the book, *We Got the Neutron Bomb: The Untold Story of L.A. Punk*.

With these stories as inspiration, the chapters that follow will unpack the experience of DIY shows, flesh out a description of the intricacies of DIY touring, and explore the various types of spaces that host punk shows. I look at how the explosion of alternative rock bands, many of which featured members who grew up on a steady diet of punk records, shifted the live music terrain. As major labels and corporate media pushed this style of music, punks moved further underground, away from the bars and clubs that once dedicated a night or two to heavier music. Instead, most punks were playing only local, or occasionally regional, shows.

House spaces are pure DIY options, requiring no real start up funds, since one's rent covers the space. They are sites of greater control for punks, at least until problems arise with neighbors, police, and landlords. Volunteer-run spaces are perhaps the ideal embodiment of punk's cultural politics, a material reflection of collective ideologies and the culture's connections to identity politics.Taken together, the events that happen in these spaces demonstrate the historical and contemporary importance of DIY punk shows to punk music and culture.

Even readers who have little to no interest in punk or in going to DIY punk shows will hopefully consider the ways in which this alternative approach to cultural production and consumption can be translated to other non-punk rock contexts. If nothing else, the next time you hear a barrage of noise blasting from a basement down the street, instead of calling the police, you can explain to your roommates or family members what's happening and why it's a good thing.

Section II

Tour Song

Career Suicide, 03/2005, Albion House, Chicago, IL

The Year DIY Broke

A mostly male crowd jumping up and down in unison to the rhythm of Sonic Youth's "Schizophrenia" is shown in slow motion. A small mosh pit breaks out on the left side of the screen. The camera doesn't focus on any one individual, but we do catch a glimpse of a guy with a wide mohawk and hooded jacket cut into a vest. He moves out of that unformed pit and toward the larger mass of bouncing bodies. A crowd surfer near the front of the stage drops back into a standing position as security guards watch the action. The black and white image switches to color and the slow motion shots transition to real-time speed as the director, David Markey, guides our focus from the crowd to the band. Sonic Youth is shot from the photographer's well in front of the stage, which provides a visual parallel to the large concert experience where bands rise above adoring fans. This footage from a festival played during Sonic Youth's 1991 one-month summer tour of Europe captures the impersonal nature of the large concert circuit.

The distance between a band and its audience is contrasted with a later scene in which Thurston Moore talks with a small group of twenty-somethings in the streets. He asks them about the state of rock and roll and then adds his own two-cents: "People see rock and roll as youth culture, and when rock and roll is monopolized by big business, what are the youth to do?" His discussants smile and look at him with a collective blank stare. "I think we should destroy the, the bogus capitalist process that is destroying youth culture by mass marketing and commercial paranoia behavior control. And the first step to do it is to destroy the record companies. Do you not agree?" The film cuts to a series of images of Sonic Youth hanging out, or possibly posing for a photo session. Kim Gordon's on-stage banter plays under this scene: "Did you know that punk rock finally broke in 1991?" she asks the audience. And with that line we've got the title of David Markey's documentary, *1991: The Year Punk Broke*, and a summary of a massive upheaval that was beginning to take shape in the U.S. as Nirvana's "Smells Like Teen Spirit" decimated hair metal's decade-long dominance of the radio airwaves and MTV's video rotation. Alternative was now mainstream and punk rock was indeed breaking, but in far more complicated ways than often discussed by critics inside and outside the punk scene.

A decade before punk supposedly broke and David Markey traveled to Europe with Sonic Youth, Nirvana, and other alternative rock bands that had recently moved from indie labels to corporate labels (e.g., Dinosaur Junior, Babes in Toyland, and Gumball), he and friend Jordan Schwartz created the *We Got Power* fanzine to perform a different type of documentation. The two punks were interested in documenting the West Coast's scenes through text and photos. David Markey and Jordan Schwartz had both recently graduated from high school and found punk to be a culture in which they could reflect on boredom, the move from adolescence to adulthood, and restless energy. The LA punk scene that provided a site of connection for a collection of weirdos was also in a state of transition from an eclectic blend of avant-garde sounds to a more unified and aggressive hardcore sound and aesthetic. Markey and Schwartz note in a two-part *Maximum Rocknroll* interview in June and July 2013 that they were part of a growing population of latchkey kids in Southern California who found a home in punk, a site to connect with others that also served as an outlet for freedom and imaginative expression. "[W]e created what we wanted to make without knowing what the rules or codes were," says David Markey. "We just had a lot energy and wanted to do stuff. Whether it was taking photos, or making films, or starting bands, or doing fanzines, or whatever; just ways to express things that were going on in our teenage head." This desire to "do stuff" materialized in a variety of ways for David Markey and Jordan Schwartz, including *We Got Power*, which was published from 1981 to 1983.

We Got Power not only modeled how to enact a belief that punks could do it themselves, but also became part of a larger body of imagery that was taking shape locally and regionally throughout the U.S. There was a range of local scenes that were forming throughout the U.S. around the same time. Those scenes consisted of active participants who started bands, made zines, organized shows, or simply showed up regularly to support what was going on. Markey's contributions to punk through the creation of *We Got Power* (in addition to co-founding the band

Sin 34) reflect this participation. But his zine and records also circulated out of Southern California to other parts of the country where punks developed some sense of what was happening on the West Coast. Those punks could then internalize some of what they saw, blend what they heard with local sounds, and ultimately make something that simultaneously cut across scenes while also helping to distinguish one scene from another. For example, Tonny Rettman's oral history of Detroit hardcore, *Why Be Something That You're Not*, features interviews with a range of people involved with Detroit's transition from proto-punk into punk and then hardcore. Band members and zine writers talk about the influence of *Flipside* and seeing the Circle Jerks. Barry Henssler from Necros adds that watching videos filmed by Corey Rusk when Rusk attended high school in LA for a year helped the Detroit kids learn to stage dive and taught them how to dress.

Many of these participants in U.S. punk in the early '80s knew about bands from other scenes via zines and/or records. Each new piece of information helped punks figure out how to be and do punk, but this knowledge was grounded in a local focus for punk's participants who, again, started their own bands, created their own zines, or tried to carve out spaces to play. As Ian MacKaye says in an interview with David Ensminger in *Left of the Dial*, "I saw things regionally. That's what I thought

Carbonas, 08/03/06, Rancho Huevos, Chicago, IL

was so cool about punk rock. I saw all these different towns had these scenes breaking out. They had their own bands, their own styles, their own way of dressing, even their own way of dancing." Ian MacKaye enjoyed these variations and was excited by the prospect of record labels mapping regional distinctions. "The idea was, we've got DC covered, Alternative Tentacles had San Francisco, Touch and Go had the Midwest, SST was doing LA. It was like, everyone do your own labels, and then we'll be a network." David Markey's early contributions to punk via *We Got Power* exemplify Ian MacKaye's hope for these regional efforts to take shape throughout the U.S.

1991: The Year Punk Broke documents bands that were representative of a rapidly transforming alternative music landscape. Some people might argue that *We Got Power* and *1991: The Year Punk Broke* are bookends, the beginning being a time when punk had no clear rules and could be shaped by participants in any ways they wanted (i.e., when punk was real and authentic) and an ending point when punk had either lost all meaning because the culture became a target for corporate culture vultures or had been seduced by new business models that radically changed the sound and experience of punk. But I think there's another story to be told, and I believe that David Markey's links to punk provide us with an entry into a discordant genealogy of a greater commitment to DIY. In fact, the supposed breaking of punk is actually a time of re-focusing on DIY punk, where punks returned to an approach that was central to the efforts of David Markey, Jordan Schwartz, and many others in the early 1980s, all of whom found punk to be wide open with infinite possibilities. The year 1991 was not an end or the beginning of an end; rather, the changes that congealed in 1991 set in motion an opportunity for punks to re-imagine what it meant to do DIY punk.

There is irony in the idea that punk broke in 1991, since punk was and remains a reaction to the limitations of mainstream political economy and culture. However, the newfound detection of punk (or punk-influenced culture) in the early 1990s by a broader mainstream audience demarcates an important transformation of underground music culture in the U.S. that has garnered a range of critical responses within punk, among popular culture critics, and by smart people who are interested in alternative culture. This collective criticism, and especially that advanced by those inside the scene, of punk's exploitation for profit, raises a host of important questions. With that said, the almost exclusive focus on mainstream forays into the underground (or the rapid increase in discourse about punk bands selling out) functioned to miss an important renewed effort in the underground. That is, even punkers were so focused on criticizing what the mainstream music business was doing that they were neglecting to critically observe the positive transformation of DIY punk as a response to mainstream interest.

There are a variety of important contributions to the emergence of a DIY touring network in the U.S. that started to solidify in the early 1990s but begin earlier. Punk shows developed in the 1980s in the context of local and regional punk identities. External and internal pressures hindered individual and collective efforts to create live music spaces; however, these strains also directly and indirectly inspired new creative approaches to organizing shows and tours. These early tours by some of punk's foundational bands set into motion a range of options for bands that followed, leading to interesting, yet problematic, ways that punk became the hot topic (all pun intended) among cultural scouts in the early 1990s.

CBGB in New York was certainly one of the best known punk venues. The club helped foster an emerging punk scene, and has been discussed in many punk histories. The widespread success of those bands contributed to an awareness of the venue among people who have little to no understanding of punk history or culture. And yet, the venue is also known by people who have little to no understanding of punk history or culture. Then there are venues that have not garnered the same level of mass cultural attention but that most punks would identify as the first semi-stable spaces where punk developed in the U.S.: Mabuhay Gardens in San Francisco, The Masque and Cathay de Grande in Los Angeles, 9:30 Club in Washington, D.C., The Rat and The Channel in Boston, Anthrax in Connecticut, and Obanion's in Chicago. All of these spaces and others faced a variety of external pressures from public officials, local residents, and the police.

Most did not last long, and, in many instances, if the venues did survive, punk gave way to a variety of other genres. I moved to New York in 1992 and saw bands at CBGB almost every week for nearly two years, but most of the bands fell into the alternative rock or indie rock categories (e.g., Unsane, Zeni Geva, Guided by Voices, Archers of Loaf). I rarely saw DIY bands there, and most of those bands had either garnered a broader buzz (e.g., New Bomb Turks) or were on their way to a major label (e.g., Quicksand). Although some punk matinees were being booked at Wetlands, most of the DIY punk bands played at the volunteer-run ABC No Rio.

Dave Zukauskas has been photographing punk bands in New England since the 1980s. He shares a similar sentiment about early DIY efforts during one of our conversations. "It took a while for people to break away from the existing infrastructure of what live music was supposed to be, an entertainment option where people go out and spend money," observes Dave. "Someone's going to make a profit, have overhead, and that sort of thing. It took a while to become its own entity that was self-run." Punks who lived in smaller towns operated without the same models, but there were far fewer options to host shows in more established spaces. Dave tells me that other than the Anthrax in Connecticut, which ran from 1982 until 1990, there weren't many DIY venues at that time.

In an effort to avoid the gaze of public officials and mainstream residents, who have historically been more concerned about any form of cultural production that they don't understand, punks in the 1980s found other venues—often in poorer parts of the city or in gay clubs or bars—where shows could be organized (e.g., La Mere Vipere and Oz in Chicago and Nunzio's in Detroit). Evading authorities only lasted for so long, and these venues soon faced mounting economic pressures often directly linked to increased problems with the police. Some punks believed that violence and destruction were at the core of the culture's essence, which affected how many people would show up and the amount of stuff in the space that was going to be destroyed.

The more mainstream bars and clubs provided a place for punks to gather and for bands to play; however, most of these venues booked punk bands in an effort to increase profits through the sale of alcohol (primarily) and via door prices (secondarily). As George Hurchalla writes in *Going Underground*, "[A] few bands with aspirations beyond the DIY punk level attempted to book shows through the more traditional rock and roll business methods." Thus, these venues were a better fit for bands that were seeking something bigger and perhaps more professional than the unstable punk spaces.

Clubs and bars that were twenty-one plus shut out underage fans, and, in theory, these venues were also unable to book bands formed by kids who were not yet twenty-one-years old. Bigger cities with a greater quantity of punks did feature more options for all-ages shows, but the trade-off was a loss of intimacy, since high-capacity venues were used. Goldenvoice, a promotion company in Southern California that booked many early punk shows and continues to promote larger alternative music concerts, booked Fender's Ballroom in Long Beach, the Santa Monica Civic Center, and the Olympic Auditorium in downtown Los Angeles. The capacity in these spaces ranged from 1,600 to 4,000 people, and the shows regularly featured a long list of punk's best-known touring and local bands. Tony Kinman from The Dils tells David Ensminger in *Left of the Dial* about the odd experience of opening for The Clash at the Santa Monica Civic Center. "It was a real rock show with real security, real backstage, real this, that, and the other," he says. "We were used to playing punk rock clubs or rented halls or stuff like that, and I was thinking, isn't this what we are supposed to destroy sort of thing?"

Big Frank Harrison was involved with the punk scene in multiple ways from very early on. He handled production for Goldenvoice, worked at Zed Records in Long Beach, and later started Nemesis Records. Big Frank notes that these larger shows were complemented by some other DIY efforts that did not happen in age-restricted bars or club venues. "John Macias, who was the singer for Circle One, used to put on shows at a place called the T-Bird Rollerdome in Whittier," he says. "It was just out and out chaos. I mean [he starts laughing] that was like stepping into a tornado and hoping that you didn't get thrown into a wall or something. It was really a crazy time."

Similar live music endeavors were taking shape throughout the U.S., as punks found ways to overcome the limited venue options by organizing shows in any place that could be put to use. Bob Suren has been an active member in the Florida punk scene for decades, running Sound Idea record store and distro, putting out records, and singing in bands. He tells me that he first heard the term "DIY" in 1988, a few years after he had been experiencing do-it-yourself punk culture. In 1985, a year or two after he got into punk rock, a friend from his high school gave Bob a flyer for a show. "He says, 'Hey, me and my friend Scott are putting on a concert.' I just thought it was awesome that a guy, who was approximately my age, was promoting a concert." Bob recognized some of the bands listed on the flyer and the rest were new to him. For Bob and other people getting into punk at that time there was a natural instinct to compare what they were doing to mainstream rock practices. "It wasn't Led Zeppelin or Aerosmith; it was eight local punk rock bands in a fire station for $3. The stage was like eighteen inches high. After the bands played they stepped off the stage and stood right next to you. One of the bands that played was three dudes from my shop class. It was just this whole other level of music that was accessible that wasn't AC/DC. You know, AC/DC were dudes touring the world in a jet plane, playing fifteen-foot high stages for 30,000 people. And there was also this level of music that I thought, 'The accessibility of it; the immediacy of it is incredible.'"

Bob says that he would hear about a show and he would make a flyer. He hadn't booked the show, found the space, nor was he playing in any of the bands. Instead, he was someone who quickly realized that anyone could contribute to the scene. The art critic David Hickey discusses how multiple music genres and art movements can be divided into two types of people: participants and spectators. "[P]articipants just appear, looking for that new thing—the thing they always wanted to see—or the old thing that might be seen anew—and having seen it, they seek to invest that thing with a new value," he writes in *Air Guitar*. "They do this simply by showing up; they do it with their body language and casual conversation[;] with written commentary, if they are so inclined[;] and their disposable income, if it falls to hand." Spectators follow trends; they show up because they think there's something to get or because they don't want to be left behind. From the very beginning, punk has been about participation and about modeling individual and collective efforts to create and share music. Participation has never been easy, though. Like those who ran official punk venues, people involved with DIY shows also experienced a range of obstacles.

In places like Stuart, Florida in the '80s there weren't clubs where punk bands could play, so the punks improvised and made use of the picnic pavilions by the beach at the Jensen Beach Causeway or the Stuart Causeway. "They were just a picnic table with a roof over it and electricity. The bands would just plug in and play there until the police showed up," claims Bob. "Sometimes they'd show up during the first band and sometimes they'd show up during the fourth band. About 99 out of 100 times the police showed up." The realistic threat of police busting shows dictated how the shows were organized. If bands wanted to increase their chance of being heard then they needed to play first. "If you were the best band on the bill, you played first. If you were the shittiest band on the bill, you played last (if you got to play at all depending on when the cops showed up)." Bob recalls attending about twenty of these pavilion shows, which highlights a level of persistence given the regularity with which shows were shut down.

Eventually the punks realized that they were not going to be able to continue at the pavilions. "We would drive out into the middle of nowhere, have these hand drawn maps of dirt roads and stuff, and we would literally play in the middle of the woods," Bob remembers. "We would get a gasoline-powered generator and 200 feet of extension chord so we could get as far away from the noise of the generator as possible. Somebody would light a bonfire and bands would play in the dirt and pine needles out in the woods. Sometimes the cops would even show up at those, which was weird. I don't know how the cops would find us in the middle of the woods."

Punk has long been linked to urban spaces and culture. Stories about the emergence of punk regularly focus on London, New York, Los Angeles, Boston. This spatial-cultural link is in part a product of urban areas having larger populations of punks, which then leads to the formation of more bands, the creation of more zines, and more people starting record labels. And cities have historically been sites where individuals have more freedom to deviate from norms. Phil from Naked Aggression notes in a 1997 *MRR* interview: "I started going to shows in '85 whenever I could get a ride into the city." He adds that "We were like a family and if someone looked punk they usually were cool and not just stupid jocks with a fresh haircut. They were radical. Punk was not socially acceptable back then. A guy with a mohawk was not on the cover of mainstream magazines. It all seemed to be a lot more underground."

Doing things like organizing shows in the woods demonstrates ingenuity and creative spirit, but it is also just taking advantage of the diverse geographic terrain of south Florida. "[T]here was a housing development in Port St. Lucie that got started—they laid the roads and started building houses—but then they stopped; it's like they went bankrupt or something," says Bob. "A bunch of bands used to play in a cul-de-sac on Becker Road. We'd just set up a generator out there and play on the asphalt until the cops showed up."

Each of the places where Bob attended shows (fire station, parkway, woods, and derelict housing development) are interesting. The suburb is often represented in fiction and news reports as a normative, safe space in which families can be protected from the social ills that plague urban centers. So many kids have formed punk bands because they want to escape the control of suburban living, yet the shows on Becker Road were imbued with the hope that this suburban cul-de-sac could shelter these punks from the authorities.

Punks in other towns didn't have to rely on the same level of guerrilla tactics that were adopted in South Florida. VFW halls, American Legion halls, and city community centers were often rented so local and regional bands could play. Sioux City Pete tells me that kids from Sioux City, Iowa and Omaha, Nebraska were able to see larger punk and metal touring bands at The Music Hall; however, most smaller DIY shows happened at the Harney Street Bingo Hall. Other than those Harney Street Bingo Hall shows "I would definitely say that the first DIY show at a community hall was a show that I put on with my friend Tim," says Pete. This May 1985 show happened at the Hinton

Community Center in Iowa, about 25 miles north of Sioux City. Pent-Up Aggression, COTC, and Discipline Problems from Des Moines, Iowa; a band from Omaha called RAF; and a local band called Malcontent played that night. Pete notes that the show happened at the Hinton Community Center "because nobody in Sioux City would rent to us. No way. It was like, 'You're fucken out of your mind. No way. Get the fuck out.'" They went to Hinton and asked if they could host a high school dance. "I was sixteen I think, maybe seventeen. They were like, 'Yeah, great.' We wore our normal clothes and lied our heads off."

Similar to the experiences of Bob in South Florida, Pete and other punks in this part of the Midwest were constantly facing pressures from the police, so he assesses the success of that show in Hinton in the context of police response. "I think they were too afraid to go in there and break it up," Pete says. "But nobody was doing anything [violent], so it was successful I guess."

There was a lengthy gap after this show because "there was no infrastructure; it was impossible." The previously mentioned Harney Street Bingo Hall was really the only option. Sometimes there would be a house show, "but they were very different animals in those days. Again, there was never a steady anything because the police would absolutely fucking shut it down. That's why we went to a place called Hinton, Iowa. You couldn't fucken put anything on in Sioux City. Already we were fucken hated by everyone."

Although police were concerned about violence connected to punk shows, there are certainly instances where the officers exacerbated the violence. Steve Macek, who is now a communication professor at North Central College, tells me about a show in Lincoln, Nebraska in December 1981 put on by Gel Productions that featured various local bands. "After a couple bands played two short sets there was a loud commotion at the back of the room and I turned and saw two huge burly cops pushing through the crowd. They walked to the front of the room and started talking to the band on stage. The organizers rushed over and the two groups had a heated exchange," Steve tells me. He says that someone announced that the show was over, and people were ushered out of the room. The problem was that the room where the bands were playing was on the second floor of a warehouse space in an older part of Lincoln. There was only one way out and the room was packed. "At least four more cops showed up with a couple of them stationing themselves near the door to the stairs. The cops then started using their extra long flashlights and billysticks to shove people fairly violently towards the exit door to the stairs. Naturally, the area around that door was clogged with people but the cops kept shoving. Eventually someone tripped and fell down on the stairs—which were wooden—and somehow one of the stairs was broken. Not only that but a water pipe under the stairs got cracked and water started flowing down the staircase. Needless to say, some people slipped and got hurt and I think (although I am not certain) that an ambulance had to be called to attend to them."

Steve says that the chaos inside the space was repeated down on the street. "The cops had cordoned off the area around the entrance to the building." The punks started taunting the cops. "I believe the words 'fascists' and 'Nazis' were shouted a few times. Several people got arrested both for refusing to exit the building and for 'failure to disperse' (which was a catch all charge always used to bust shows)." Steve explains that the police claimed that the show was shut down for a fire code violation and a ticket was issued to the punks from Gel, who then had to organize another benefit show to raise the funds to pay the fine.

Pete notes that violence was a major problem in the 1980s Sioux City-Omaha scene. "Shows would get shut down all the time. And to be honest, we fucken deserved it. We'd go in and fucken wreck their hall." His description of the chaos at these shows is similar to Big Frank's summary of the wild energy at the T-Bird Rollerdome. The Rollerdome shows were happening in Southern California, but the kids in Iowa (and elsewhere) were mimicking what they perceived to be some kind of hardcore essence that they discovered via fanzine descriptions of the Southern California scene, records coming out of that part of the country (both the sound and the visual cues provided via inserts), and Penelope Spheeris' *The Decline of Western Civilization* documentary. "I admit that a lot of it with me and my mates was a misinterpretation of what we thought the LA scene was 'cause of all the violence glorified in *The Decline*. In hindsight, I understand that a lot of that stuff isn't what punk rock was all about, but this is said from the eyes of a 45-year-old man. As a 15-year-old little fucker, we were like, 'What the fuck, man?' We wanted to light everything up. So it was a mix of us being fucking idiots and the authorities going, 'What the fuck!'"

Pete and his friends weren't alone when it came to using *The Decline* as a punk rock guide for living. Darren Walters, co-owner of Jade Tree Records, writes about this in the edited collection, *My First Time*: "Sure we had seen The Cure and other such acts at big arenas, and interacted with others of our kind, but what we were craving was the kind of show that we saw in *Decline of the Western Civilization* or *Suburbia*." Blake Schwarzenbach, singer and guitarist from Jawbreaker, Jets to Brazil, and The Forgetters, notes in the same collection that seeing *The Decline* was a surrogate for his first show. Reflecting on that experience years later, he realized that the film "suggested there was a place to go, even if the place it showed had already been condemned or evicted or had fled." The dystopic narrative of *The Decline* "heralded a new beginning, by destroying everything that was false and saying we don't need your help or patronage."

Although Pete highlights how the kids in his scene contributed to their own problems, he is also well aware of added pressures living in a smaller city where police and public officials were less tolerant of difference. "Some of it was unacceptable to begin with. Iowa and Nebraska are not LA. You couldn't go to Hollywood. Going to California was like going to fucking Mars. There was nothing around." Of course, as we see in a range of histories of punk in major cities, police were not tolerant in those cities either. Dem Hopkins who ran Oz, a punk club in Chicago that started in the late '70s, talked about struggles with the police during a panel session I organized at DePaul University about punk in Chicago in the '80s. He noted that being a punk in Chicago at that time was a constant struggle. Dem recounted a situation where he was picked up by police, held overnight, let go in the morning, and picked up again as he walked from the police station to his home.

It is likely that police pressure happened in concert with a broader official approach to treating punks as criminals, which had the effect of limiting venue options. "Early '80s Chicago was a weird place," Ben Pierce told me. He played in various punk bands in Chicago in the 1980's and claims that, even though Chicago is "such a huge city, there weren't that many places to play. This continued even after the punk/hardcore heyday, and into the late '80s. Despite that, there also wasn't really a network of non-club spaces either." Ironically, the basement of Hemenway Church in Evanston (a suburb just north of Chicago) became one place where they could do occasional punk shows. "There was a youth group kinda deal called YOU (Youth Organization Umbrella, I think) that the church put in charge of renting it out." Ben was involved with organizing a few of those shows. He says that at "one point the church decided it didn't want its floors scuffed up so instituted a 'no shoes' policy. We did at least one more show there after that, which we fittingly dubbed the 'Punk Rock Sock Hop.' The bill was Rights of the Accused, Nadsat Rebel (my band at the time), and one or two others. This was '84 or '85."

Although there are some church spaces that have been used to host punk shows, this type of space is certainly less common. And some punks would argue that doing a show in a church runs counter to a punk ethos, since organized religion is one of the central sites of critique in punk music and culture. Sioux City Pete and his crew didn't have access to a space like this, and they were quickly running out of community spaces as well. "We tried to have another show six months after the Hinton show, at this place in Sioux City but there was this riot," says Pete. "I can't remember who was at that show; I just remember getting beat down by cops. But we were like, 'Well, I don't think we're going to be able to rent any community centers anymore.'" In the late 1980s Tim Archer found a more permanent option in the form of a basement gymnasium in a former school. He asked Pete about helping put on shows in this space, which they named Kings Court. "Basically this guy that was a junk collector and had a junk pawn shop and a piss-ass wino bar—the worst bar ever. We were like, 'Can we rent your basement for whatever?' And he was like, 'Yeah!' It was fucken lawless; it was completely lawless in every way. It was definitely do-it-yourself, more do-it-yourself than anyone could fucken imagine: total piece of shit PA [public-address system]. 'PA. What's a PA? Who cares.'" These shows happened until 1989 "and then you can take a guess about what happened: a riot."

The violence that played out in various scenes was a topic of heated debate among punks, splintering scenes and likely leading a segment of some scenes to give up on live shows. Some punks considered this aggression as a mirror image of mainstream actions and norms that punk was supposed to be rejecting. Others understood that there was a difference between problematic violence by punks directed at other punks and more acceptable forms of violence as represented by conflicts between punks and the State.

Ironically, violence at shows might have indirectly contributed to bonding among bands from different scenes and facilitating some early touring networks. Michael Azerrad writes in the chapter about Black Flag in *Our Band Could Be Your Life*: "[T]he violence became too much for the police and the community. If Black Flag was to keep playing shows, they'd have to play them out of town. But back then literally only a handful of American indie punk bands undertook national tours." The arena rock band was the model for touring, but punk bands weren't going to play sold out arenas. Punk bands tended not to think beyond their local or regional scenes. Yeah, the Sex Pistols had toured the U.S., The Ramones toured some, and many of the bands that have been retroactively identified as proto-punk toured, but these bands still had one foot in more mainstream approaches to the music business (managers and booking agents in addition to possibly receiving tour support from their major labels). Hardcore communities developed DIY show options grounded in localism, but lacked a model for national touring. Black Flag helped re-map the punk touring landscape. "[T]here were few cities besides New York, L.A., and Chicago that had clubs that would even book punk rock bands," writes Azerrad about the early touring circuit. "The solution was to tour as cheaply as possible and play anywhere [Black Flag] could--anything from a union hall to someone's rec room. They didn't demand a guarantee or accommodations or any of the

Cap'n Jazz, 12/22/94 Jon Hiltz House, NJ

usual prerequisites, and they could survive that way—barely, anyway."

Black Flag's approach to touring—on the road for months on end, playing wherever they could get gigs, establishing new networks among punk bands and fans—has become one of the central features of hardcore's genesis narrative. Henry Rollins' tour diary, *Get in the Van*, released almost a decade after the Rollins-fronted version of the band stopped touring, affirmed and expanded that tale. Azerrad argues, "The band's selfless work ethic was a model for the decade ahead, overcoming indifference, lack of venues, poverty, even police harassment." His temporal frame of "the decade ahead" is connected to the larger argument he advances in his book about indie rock bands finding success in the 1990s because the punk bands of various stripes laid the groundwork in the 1980s. Necros, Minor Threat, The Misfits, Circle Jerks, The Effigies, D.R.I and many others that are now considered foundational U.S. hardcore bands started to tour after Black Flag showed that punk bands could leave their hometowns. But smaller bands that played shows attended by Bob Suren, Sioux City Pete, Ben Pierce, and thousands of other punks throughout the U.S. rarely saw national touring as an option in the mid-1980s.

Azerrad is right to point out that independent rock bands with varying degrees of connection to DIY punk scenes were quicker to see touring as important and as do-able. One of those bands was Nirvana. Ironically, their success would indirectly lead punks to reconsider what it meant to do DIY, but first these bands had to figure out what it meant to be punk amidst a new level of corporate attention directed at punk.

Many of the best-known foundational punk and post-punk bands are connected to major labels in the U.S. (e.g., Velvet Underground and The Stooges in the late '60s; The Ramones, The Clash, Sex Pistols in the mid-'70s; Siouxsie and the Banshees, The Cure, and The Jesus and Marychain in the '80s). Some of these bands became affiliated with major labels when their UK labels licensed records to corporations in the U.S., and others signed with larger independents that were soon bought by a major. Additionally, there had been failed major label distribution deals for some of hardcore's foundational bands. For example, Black Flag signed a deal with Unicorn/MCA to distribute *Damaged,* and I.R.S. Records briefly distributed Dead Kennedys' *Fresh Fruit for Rotting Vegetables* (through A&M). And some of the most critically acclaimed independent rock bands that emerged from the punk scene, such as Husker Du and The Replacements, left their indie labels to sign with corporate labels in the mid-to-late 1980s. In short, the seeds for the mainstream discovery of punk in the early 1990s were sown much earlier. The major sea change in the early 1990s was the volume of punk or punk-influenced bands that were signed by corporations and the expectation that these bands could become the next mega groups.

Nirvana's mass success inspired a general sense amidst certain segments of various independent music scenes that there were greater possibilities to reach larger audiences that had become hungry for more discordant sounds and a different type of cultural politics than the slick excess of 1980s mainstream metal. Similarly, the corporate record labels were on a feeding frenzy in search of the next Nirvana. Major label Artists & Repertoire (A&R) reps began paying more attention to college radio playlists; scouring the indie scenes in Boston, Chapel Hill, Champaign-Urbana, Chicago, Seattle, San Diego, and other places; and looking to fanzine writers for clues about underground bands that might reach a broader audience. Meanwhile, label presidents reached beyond their A&R departments by doing deals with independent labels for two-tiered production and distribution options (i.e., CDs would be distributed through the corporate "independent" distribution network, and if the record reached some pre-determined level of sales or garnered enough buzz then the major label would pick up promotion and distribution). Music corporations also started offshoot labels that could appear to be independent, even opening small offices separate from the corporate headquarters, but were completely funded by the major label (e.g., Seed Records, Revolution Records, Vernon Yard). Bands who had not been around long enough to put out more than a 7" and/or get much attention from music-focused fanzines became targets by these music giants. In fact, Thurston Moore's call for the destruction of corporate record labels in *1991: The Year Punk Broke* contradicted Sonic Youth's actions, since the band not only released records through DGC but also worked as scouts for/business partners with DGC through the band's Ecstatic Peace label. The signing of the bands Cell and St. Johnny were a product of that relationship.

Three years after punk supposedly broke, another wave of major label punk signings began with Green Day. The success of *Dookie* inspired talent scouts seeking the next Nirvana to shift their focus from grunge to pop punk and post-hardcore. Once again, labels sought to mimic a success story. Geffen signed Jawbreaker and Girls Against Boys; Atlantic added Jawbox, Samiam, Civ, and Bad Religion to the roster; Shudder to Think signed with Epic; Drive Like Jehu and Rocket from the Crypt were signed by Interscope; and The Offspring moved from Epitaph to Columbia. Corporate labels considered street cred to be a foundation for breaking a band via more mainstream radio and video channels. This approach to success rarely came to fruition since most bands could not sell enough to make back the personal and recording advances paid by the major labels to do the deals.

Thomas Frank notes in his essay, "Alternative to What?" from the *Commodify Your Dissent* collection, that punk was merely the latest countercultural form to be sucked into a moneymaking machine, watered down for middle-of-the-road palatability, and shot into the larger commercial marketplace for mainstream consumption. "There are few spectacles corporate America enjoys more than a good counterculture, complete with hairdos of defiance, dark complaints about the stifling 'mainstream,' and expensive accessories," writes Frank. Punk had been on the radar of most mainstream media industries since the late '70s, but most execs believed punk was "commercially unviable" for a variety of reasons, including the "difficult sound." The rise of alternative rock in the late 1980s provided the mainstream marketplace with a way into alternative culture without having to deal with the radical politics and discordant sounds. And the companies could follow through on the major discovery in the 1960s by advertisers that anti-establishment themes can be used in marketing campaigns to convince consumers to consider replacing outdated, no longer hip clothes, records, and other identity-shaping goods with new stuff.

In his *New Yorker* article, "The Cool Hunt" (the seeds of the book, *The Tipping Point*), Malcolm Gladwell describes how the selling of cool begins with a quest to find and exploit cultural life that exists below the proverbial radar. Gladwell develops his analysis through a description of two women who work as marketing executives and are considered forerunners in the adoption of cool hunting as a technique for product development and market testing. He explains that trends move from innovators--hip kids who do what they want, how they want, and when they want--through a series of early adopters, and then into the mainstream. The trick, Gladwell's interviewees note, is to find the cool people, not the cool things, because the things will always change as cool

Iconoclast, 8/11/93 Roseville Statue, Sacramento, CA

people's interests are modified. Cool people will always spot cool things. Of course, it takes one to know one, and if the companies are going to discover the next shopping mall-bound trend then cool people need to do the hunting. As with the punk bands that signed with corporate labels, some innovators want to be found for myriad reasons, whereas others change up what they do to elude mainstream attention. Gladwell identifies this rule of cool as the quicker the chase, the quicker the flight, suggesting that some cool people don't want to be found. Although Gladwell's piece was written after Nirvana had become a household name, he describes an approach to seeking out alternative cultures that pre-date the discovery of punk. And in the post-Nirvana age this quest for cool meant that all things punk should be on the radar of cool hunters of various stripes, from fashion consultants to sneaker executives to major label A&R reps.

Although some punks were excited by this new opportunity to make money and gain attention, the majority found the corporate patrolling of the underground scene to exist on a spectrum of problematic—from mildly irritating to openly wounded to pissed off. Most notable among the responses was a corporate business themed issue of *Maximum RocknRoll* in June 1994 that focused on major labels and other corporate influences that impacted punk.

Tim Yohannan began the issue with an argument about a history of threats to punk, reminding readers that in 1988 his column in *MRR* described the general negative influence of skinheads in the scene: beating up bands, destroying punk clubs, and fighting with zine editors. He called readers' attention to slight changes in his language to reflect the current crisis faced by the punk scene, replacing "skinheads" with "major labels" and descriptions of physical violence with illustrations of economic violence: "Within the last two years, major labels have bought up at least 50 underground bands, have undermined punk clubs and bought their way into radio programs[;] have bought off zine editors, label owners and indie distributors. They threaten to stifle and ultimately control this community, and little is being done to resist this threat."

As can be expected, the wave of interest in punk bands among major label scouts came to a grinding halt when sales rarely matched expectations. A&R reps turned their attention to manufactured boy bands, pop acts, and more mainstream sounding rock and rap artists. By the end of the 1990s, radical shifts in the production and sale of music meant that punk bands were rarely a priority for corporate labels, although the corporations still found ways to get a piece of the proverbial pie through their so-called independent distribution companies. The doomsday scenario that seemed to undergird Tim Yo's column didn't come to fruition, but his concerns about the inventible major label betrayal and exploitation of the underground made sense.

Thomas Frank advanced a similar argument about the importance of independent music, advocating for two central responses that the underground should consider in the face of corporate interest: (1) lie to marketing types and (2) just say "no". The first approach is in line with a history of tactics designed to disrupt mainstream cultural values and a capitalist imperative. I am thinking about a variety of radical performances of the Situationist International and efforts by the Yippees (e.g., trying to levitate the Pentagon). But the second move—to just say no to mainstream cultural production and consumption—is more important, because shunning mainstream interest was at the core of creating a DIY touring network in the U.S. in the mid-1990s that continues in the present. Punks were faced with a choice: mirror the approaches of the mainstream music industry when it came to putting out records, touring, and interacting with underground media or revisit some of the successes that took shape in the 1980s, expanding the DIY spirit that led people to book shows in beach pavilions, out in the woods, in community halls and to keep going when faced with a range of external and internal challenges. But if punk was to continue to push boundaries aesthetically while growing a community of like-minded punks, it was important that those local efforts expanded into a broader DIY network. In the end, punk broke, but the term "broke" has a range of meanings depending on one's standpoint: punk became mainstream, punk splintered, punk opened up and spread out. This last sense of the term fits with my own conceptions of DIY punk post-Nirvana. The temporary mainstream infatuation with punk instigated reconsideration of how DIY could be done.

With a Little Help from Our Friends

There are roughly 130 people crammed into a basement that should hold about 35. It's summer and the weather outside is hot, so it's scorching in here. That heat is made more intense by the steady movement of sweaty bodies trying to keep up with the blistering pace of Coke Bust. The basement at Coach House, a space that was used for a handful of shows before becoming another house on a list of the disappeared, is L-shaped. Coke Bust is set up in the corner where the L intersects. A wooden pole a few feet in front of the band seems to have a magical magnetic force, pulling the people who are dancing. They grab the pole, spin around, and then smash or fall into others in the chaotically formed pit. I am standing next to the stairs to the right of the pit and along the extended part of the L. The stairs appear to lead to an apartment, or maybe a coach house. Those of us situated next to the stairs repeatedly push back against the crush of bodies that ebb and flow at us like waves crashing on a beach. A skinny white guy who is about five-foot-six figures out that he can climb up the outside of the steps and jump onto the people in the pit, so in addition to negotiating the flow of moving bodies we also need to start shifting our heads so we don't get kicked when he jumps over us. I look to my left and behind me. Bodies throughout the basement move every which way and yet move as one.

Each scene features its own unique way of responding to different punk sub-genres. Hardcore and some power-violence bands inspire more chaotic forms of participation in Chicago. Pop punk and post-hardcore shows might appear to be less frenzied because the dancing does not seem to be as aggressive; however, the movement in the space combines with the lack of distance between the bands and the punks who come to see the bands to generate a different kind of passionate energy. Guitarists are pressed up against the amps. Photographers and videographers stand behind the drummer to avoid blurry art caused by repeated bumping. Singers have microphones pushed away from their mouths. Punks sometimes have mics handed to them so they can sing. This is not how most people experience live music. The more things seem to feel right for the people in a DIY space, the more dangerous or unusual things would likely appear to be to

those outside the scene.

The barriers that shield us from others, or what sociologist Georg Simmel referred to as a "blasé attitude," give way to a shared togetherness in DIY spaces: sweat, singing, movement. This collective interaction in the DIY show space materializes the philosophical ideals that undergird punk. That is, what takes shape at the DIY punk show space is the culmination of some core goals about the way punk can be collectively created and felt. The show experience serves as the landing point for a broad-based DIY punk touring circuit. Local DIY shows and DIY tours exist within a longer history of doing DIY. Current DIY efforts grow from, but also help re-imagine, the traditions of organizing shows that began in the 1980s and shifted dramatically after punk broke in the early 1990s. Bands and promoters continue a tradition within DIY punk in which people compare the experiences of their local scenes (both positive and negative dynamics) and shared approaches to making things happen that cut across different scenes. Networks of trust are formed among punks as they interact regionally and nationally, reflecting desires to be together economically, socially, culturally, and politically in ways that deviate from mainstream norms.

The corporate interest in punk from the early 1990s through the middle of that decade had a complicated influence on DIY punk. From one perspective, bands and labels developed more sophisticated forms of promotion and expanded their avenues for distribution as they impersonated major labels. This new approach to business meant that kids living in areas without college radio or local fanzines might learn about punk when prior to the 1990s they were unlikely to come across the music. They could find Rancid or Texas is the Reason or Fugazi and then discover that a whole world of underground music existed by reading interviews with these bands in alternative rock music magazines or via CD liner notes, checking out label mates of these bands, or because these bands would tour with good opening bands that were now seen by the kids. But mostly the influence of the mainstream industry was like a virus, introducing an element of greed, foregrounding fame as a foundational value, and offering a business model focused on music as a product that should yield large profits. This incorporation of punk into a mainstream system, or punk businesses mimicking corporate practices, ran counter to core tenets upon which punks have historically defined themselves. As Stephen Duncombe argues in his book *Notes from Underground*, negative identity is a key concept for understanding any alternative culture. In Duncombe's analysis, zine makers—and this can be extended to punks in general—think about their own identities in opposition to more mainstream ways of being in the world. Rejecting the values that guide the straight world (money, beauty, fame, power) is one important way that people self-identify as a punk. Such individual beliefs are then collectively enacted. The sociologist Joseph Gusfield notes in *Community: A Critical Response* that distinctions between "us" and "them" help group members gain some sense of belonging and self-identification and by extension, form communities.

This division between DIY punk ("us") and mainstream industry practices ("them") extended beyond music distribution and promotion strategies. Another key difference was, and remains, in the area of touring. DIY punk bands book their own shows. They map out the best possible tour given the available dates, which are often influenced by work or school schedules. Usually one person in the band takes the lead by contacting people who book houses, volunteer-run spaces, or other locales. Or the touring band will contact bands they like and try to organize a show together while relying on the local bands' contacts. E-mail, message boards, social media messaging, and phone calls are the primary communication options for connecting with people who book shows at DIY spaces. The touring band is usually paid based on the number of people who show up. Some promoters will give all of the money to the touring band while others set aside some of the money to pay local bands. If the show is in a house then the promoter is unlikely to keep any cash, whereas shows in community spaces often have added expenses (e.g., a promoter needs to rent a community hall or a non-profit volunteer-run space needs to cover rent and utilities). The bands are usually paid after the rental fees are covered, which might also include a PA and a sound person, or based on a pre-arranged split of the door price.

Non-DIY touring features booking agents who map out the tours, request a payment guarantee (i.e., the band is going to be paid an agreed-upon amount no matter how many people purchase tickets or pay an entry fee to see the band), and then collect a percentage of that guarantee. Contracts are signed by the booking agent and show promoters. A band with more negotiating power can set ticket prices, often has a variety of riders that range from sensible requests like food and water to the extreme, and will get a percentage in addition to the guarantee after a certain amount of tickets are sold. The venue might also take a piece of the band's merchandise sales, which is one reason why prices are so high for T-shirts, posters, and other gear compared to buying this same merch from a band in a DIY space. Smart booking agents and thoughtful promoters both have an understanding of the band's status and the general trends of a specific market, and can then make choices about venue size.

Some agents work exclusively with bands that play clubs and bars throughout the U.S. Other agents have a diverse client roster that consists of bands that play smaller bars or clubs, bands that play medium-sized spaces, and bands that play larger venues. Similarly, there are promoters that exclusively book punk bands. Some promoters might have started out doing punk shows but moved to larger alternative music concerts or festivals. In general, the mainstream business model is presented as a system that allows bands to focus on music while other people

handle the business (booking agents, lawyers, managers, road managers, and the like). From one perspective, this explanation of an art/business division makes sense since artists shouldn't be bogged down with complications surrounding T-shirt orders or trying to assess if a promoter is going to do a good job; however, this approach also means that there are a variety of people influencing how the music is made and shared and then taking a (large) piece of the financial pie. Just as various independent bands were pushed into the spotlight in the early- to mid-1990s, so were booking agents, promoters, and managers who had up until that point been part of an extended circle of friends helping out a band or scene.

It is rare for people who book DIY punk shows now to work with booking agents, but some punks regularly coordinated with agents when the touring circuit was developing in the early-1990s. "We did Offspring and their guarantee was $400," Dan Dittmer, who booked shows in Rapid City, South Dakota, tells me. "Stormy Shepard was their booking agent. She would call me: 'Dan, I've got these guys and I'll fax you over their rider.' And I'm like, 'Stormy, you know we can't do that. They get the usual: food at the house, have a good time, a place to stay, wash clothes, and we're all good.' She says that she knows: 'X off everything and initial it and fax it back, I'll initial it, and we'll be good.'" This is obviously before the Offspring blew up. Dan says that a large majority of the bands, including the Offspring, understood that shows he booked at that time did not have a guarantee. He would do everything he could to promote the show and then work hard to make sure that the show ran smoothly.

Dan's comment about guarantees and riders reflects the main reason why DIY show promoters don't work with booking agents. The issue is not the booking agent per se; rather, when a band uses a booking agent, it is commonly understood that a guarantee is expected. Guarantees not only create a base level of pay for the band, but also insure some income for the agent. This wasn't always the case, but as punk bands found mainstream success in the mid-1990s, their business practices changed. "Back then it really was just punk rock, fly by the seat of my pants and it was for the bands, too. A lot of these bands weren't big yet, so they were learning what they could ask and not ask for," Terry Taylor says to me. Terry started booking shows in garages and parks in Sioux Falls, South Dakota when he was fifteen. He later found a steady space for a few years at a community hall called Nordic Hall before moving to a club. "Stormy's a good example. She booked a lot of the Revelation, Epitaph, and Fat Wreck Chords bands and as those bands got bigger, she started asking for guarantees." Terry notes that "the high end guarantees were probably $300" for the bigger bands. "Once you got a few shows under your belt and realized that you could do almost any show and count on minimum 200 people, but usually 200-400 people, you felt comfortable doing that [guarantee]."

It is interesting to note, though, that many of the first wave of DIY promoters in the early '90s modeled their approach to show promotion after mainstream companies. The scene reports and the "Book Your Own Fuckin' Tour" section listings in *MRR* at that time were littered with listings for various "Production" companies (Splat Productions!, Dead End Productions, Amino Caravan Productions) even if many of these companies were really just single-person operations.

Most DIY promoters doing shows today would have a hard time imagining regular shows that draw 200-400 people. Therefore, it's important to stop here for a moment to contextualize these claims about attendance figures. The explosion of alternative music in the U.S. shaped national touring networks and local show success. Terry's experiences in Sioux Falls were not a

statistical anomaly. "We got on average of 200-400 people for shows because of Nirvana. From late '91 to early '93 it was fucken insane," Sioux City Pete tells me about King's Court. "It didn't matter who the bands were. It could have been a band I was playing in or a local band or L7 or whatever. Hundreds of people, mostly kids, heard grunge and it changed their lives."

Although these successes provided opportunities for DIY promoters to bring touring bands to local scenes and for the touring bands to connect with people throughout the U.S., the broader awareness of punk created some problems for some promoters. By the mid-to-late 1990s punk promoters were contacted by booking agents and people at record labels with a skewed sense of local scenes and did not seem to understand the history of DIY show promotion. These industry people were using mainstream touring practices as a model for their touring punk bands (or so-called punk bands). Similarly, bands started to think that success in large cities should translate across scenes. "We were getting calls from Tooth and Nail [a medium sized Christian punk label distributed by Sony with eight gold albums] and stuff like that," Dan Dittmer says to me, "and they'd be like, 'This band wants to play and we need $500 and we need this and we need that.' And I would go, 'I'm gonna be up front with you: we'll guarantee them $100 and after that if they make more, we'll be more than happy to give them more. We're gonna give them a place to stay; it's real grassroots.' But no, they have to

Shoppers, 10/16/11, Flywheel, Easthampton, MA

have a Ramada and they have to have clean towels and a veggie tray or three cases of beer or whatever the fuck their rider was. And I was like, 'Dude, it's not gonna happen.' But the guy is just arguing with me. I ask, 'Have you been to South Dakota?' and he says, 'No.' So I tell him, 'Don't tell me what my scene is like.'"

Jordan Brand, who booked shows in Omaha, Nebraska starting in 1997, explains, "I was very up front with booking agents about this: 'I am not a promoter who is making a living from this,'" Jordan tells me. "I would explain that this percentage goes to the band and this percentage goes to the venue to keep in operation." At the time Jordan was booking a volunteer-run space called Cog Factory, noting that 35 percent of the door went to the Cog and 65 percent to the bands. "My whole reason I was doing this was because I liked these bands and I wanted them to play my town."

The 1990s punk bubble burst and crowd sizes at punk shows decreased. The DIY punk promoters who had been booking during that time and continued to book returned to the approaches to live music upon which punk scenes were built, viewing the guarantee as a rock star demand that places undue burden on the local scene. If the band lacks the reputation to draw enough people to meet the financial requirements of the guarantee, then the show promoter has to pull money out of her or his pocket to cover the band's guarantee. However, some bookers will pay a guarantee in some situations. Zach Weeks, who is in the band Lovechild and books shows in Boston, tells me that a band that is well known enough to play the large room at Democracy Center (a volunteer-run community space that does punk shows on weekends) would bring enough people to meet a guarantee. "I work with a few booking agents—I use that term very loosely—and their bands will have a guarantee. And again, I use that term very loosely. But if you have a show coming through that's going to draw 100 kids easily, will at least draw 100 kids, you won't have a problem paying a band $250."

The decisions of DIY promoters to avoid booking agents and of bands to refrain from requesting guarantees are not simply a product of individual likes and dislikes; rather, current DIY promoters and touring bands mostly understand that show attendances will be erratic. Additionally, these business choices exist in a historical context in which we find overarching and long-running conversations among punks about what DIY should mean and how a DIY philosophy can be enacted. Current bands and promoters will have varying degrees of knowledge about this history but at minimum they are implicitly continuing an important tradition of adopting and carrying out an alternative economic and social model for touring and show promotion.

As most people involved in punk know, though, specific actions and choices in the scene tend to emerge from on-going heated debates. The next room filled with punks who are in total agreement about something will be the first room filled with punks who are in total agreement about something. In an October 2011 *MRR* guest column RD makes a persuasive argument that the DIY approach to touring in the U.S. ultimately hurts the bands. RD claims that the standard DIY tour experience includes getting paid $50, not being offered any food or a place to sleep, and having to save as much money as possible prior to the tour to cover the costs of being on the road. "There are two attitudes about DIY hardcore/punk that I've encountered," writes RD. "There's the U.S. 'DIY for the punxxx fuck guarantees fuck rock stars you fuckin' posers' attitude. And then there's the

Boilerman, 06/04/13, 86 Mets, Chicago, IL

European 'Let's do as much as we can to help our own' attitude. Guess which one I like more." Touring in the U.S., like touring in Europe, brings people together in a communal manner, but does so in ways that raise a host of questions about economics, travel, and social connection. "In Europe it was not uncommon for us to get 200 or more Euros a day, a very comfortable sleeping place, dinner, and then breakfast in the morning, and sometimes unlimited beer or some hash." RD notes that pay in poorer countries was still better than most shows in the U.S. Europe also features an added bonus of short drives between shows. "But then we all know the situation here. Drive nine hours to get to a decrepit 'punk' house where everyone's beyond experimenting with some hard drug and they tell you all the local bands canceled and they don't know if anyone's coming but you can crash on the floor in the living room if you really need to and as long as you don't mind the hypodermic needles. Maybe I'm exaggerating but you know what I mean."

RD describes a friend in Paris who does guarantees for every show and keeps all money beyond the guarantee. She sets aside the extra funds for shows that she expects to draw smaller crowds but she still wants to book. This approach to booking is clearly more focused on a belief that each show helps shape a scene rather than treating a single show as disconnected from what comes before and after. In an *Anti-Matter Anthology* interview with Norman Brannon, Ian MacKaye describes this same general context of specific shows fitting into a larger whole. "We'll work with these younger promoters who usually do shows for like 50 people, or who usually end up running to their bank machines to pay the bands. So when they do a show with us and we'll generate $2,000 to $3,000 or more, I'll do the split and I'll hand them a chunk of money," says Ian MacKaye. "They'll be like, 'Fuck, I don't want this money. I don't want to think about having all this money.' It's crazy. I'll say, 'Look, all this time you've been bringing bands here where you lost money on gigs ... You don't mind giving away money? Take the money, put it in a box, bring a band here. If you lose some money, don't go to the bank machine. Go to the box.'" Fugazi was working at a level that is beyond what most DIY bands experience now. These DIY bands will need two or three tours to see $2,000 to $3,000, not a single show. But the issue Ian MacKaye raises is crucial: bands and promoters need to think beyond single shows and instead consider all shows as contributions to a larger effort to make a scene. "That's the whole point: You reinvest in the community. I just wish the independent promoters would take advantage of this access to cash."

RD's discussion of good paydays in Europe and Ian MacKaye's encouragement of promoters to keep door money can appear to emphasize commerce over and against art. But the purity/sell out dichotomy is overly simplistic because punk's relationship to capitalism is complicated. "So, does this sound like I'm/we're asking too much[?]" asks RD. "If so, I have a couple important questions for you. How much do you actually like this band? And if you think they're just whatever, why are you bothering to do their show then?" This general framing of the European and U.S. touring contexts leads RD to the ways that the guarantee reflects where DIY promoters stand when it comes to truly supporting bands. "What the fuck is so wrong with a guarantee?" The guarantee can inspire some level of a working partnership, claims RD. "If you negotiated with a band to say $150, maybe that would motivate you to actually do your fucking job as a promoter/dude doing the show/whatever you call it and actually collect $5 each from 30 people. Just 30 people. Seriously, I think I could call up my friends, tell them about the show and

have them bring some friends too and get at least 30 people. When it's left to just giving a band 'whatever' there's not much motivation."

The question about why a promoter does a show if he or she "thinks the band is just whatever" is a good place to start because the query takes us back to the point at which a band is booked. RD suggests that promoters should only book bands that they love because that interest will motivate maximum show promotion efforts. The issue raised when RD challenges promoters' motivations reflects some heated and on-going conversations among punks involved with doing shows about quality promotion and show saturation. RD believes the guarantee will inspire true promotion compared to simply booking the show and waiting for the band to arrive. There are instances when a person books a show to help out a band, but isn't really into the band. For example, Jeremy Smith from Flywheel, a volunteer-run space in Western Massachusetts, tells me about "rogue shows" Flywheel did in the past. "[W]e would get tons of bands emailing us each week. We would have these shows that weren't curated by someone but facilitated by a Flywheel booker who had no interest in the bands. They're like, 'Oh, we think these bands look good. We think some people would be into them, so let's book this show.' But there was no motivation for the booker to promote the show." Jeremy says that bookers would do these rogue shows because they wanted to help fill out programming and contribute to a more diverse calendar at Flywheel. "But those shows don't really happen anymore and those are always risky shows to do. It's nice to be able to help a band out on tour but I'm not really interested in sitting around and listening to a band that I'm not interested in for four hours and then I have to get up for work the next morning."

Zack Furness, who is a communication professor and has played in multiple punk bands says to me that part of the problem is a shift toward Internet promotion. Promoters "figure, 'I posted something on Facebook, so if people come, they come.' That doesn't usually cut it as far as putting on shows." That lack of promotional sense can extend to the ways a promoter runs a show. For example, Jim Gies from the band Boilerman tells me, "We played this show in North Carolina. We showed up and there was no one at the house except for this young sixth or seventh grade kid and he had to go to choir practice. He left us alone in the house; the promoter wasn't there until like twenty minutes later. We find out that their PA is a little combo, a little karaoke PA that's fifteen watts. He said, 'We don't have a mic or a power cord for it.' We played in this little kitchen. There were no other local bands, of course, and after we played he said: 'Boilerman's on tour so give them some money.' People whip their wallets out while we're breaking down. I thought he was going to go outside and collect their money on the way out. They didn't know where to give their money and he just went outside and smoked a cigarette and hung out with his friend or whatever. People didn't know who to give the money to so they just left." Boilerman was booked because the promoter liked the band—he reached out to Jim to do the show, Jim didn't contact him—but sometimes liking the band isn't enough; some show promoters either don't know what they're doing or run into problems that derail a show.

If promoters only booked bands they loved, there would be a lot fewer shows. Some punks who live in places with active scenes might believe that fewer shows could counter smaller attendances caused by a saturation of live music, which would also help overcome a less energized vibe in the spaces on any given day. Patrick Houdek, who ran a compilation tape label in the late 1980s and was involved with booking early shows at Lost Cross in Carbondale, Illinois, continues to photograph punk bands. "At Fireside Bowl they weren't having shows seven days a week, but sometimes they had two shows a night," he tells me.

"With all of those out-of-town bands you need opening bands. I think there were too many bands that probably shouldn't have played yet."

If shows decrease in quantity, it would be more difficult for younger bands to play out and get experience. The new bands would likely suffer most since promoters will want to go with bands they already know via an existing friendship or because an established band is likely to help with the overall draw. Again, Patrick Houdek tells me that once Lost Cross started having regular shows (moving from one or two a month to shows almost every weekend), people started saying that they didn't want to pay, even when it was $2 for a show featuring touring bands. Instead, these punks just wanted to hang out on the porch.

Felix Havoc writes in his January 2004 *MRR* column, "It's harder than ever to sell records or get people to turn up to shows for all but a handful of very popular or hyped bands. A big part of this is the general lowering of the bar across the board for what is credible material to release and tour on in the punk/hardcore scene," writes Felix. "[F]ew bands seem to be able to hold an audience rapt with sheer power song after song. I hate to be so negative in an era when much hardcore *is* being made, but it seems the audience continues to contract rather than grow as people are unwilling to gamble on records or shows that they think might not be worth their time and money."

The quantity of bands playing might make it hard to support local and touring bands, but the live show remains a crucial feature of punk culture. Even less aggressive-sounding forms of punk (e.g., death rock) are more raucous than most other genres of music and that energy is best experienced live and with other punks. Therefore, a band might be booked because the promoter knows that people in the scene want to see different bands (even though fewer people will show up than if a well-known band was playing) and the band's live show creates a buzz. Dan Dittmer says to me that the first time Lifetime and Resurrection played in Rapid City, there might have been 30 people in attendance. Those people were so impressed by both bands that they told everyone in the scene about the show. The next time each band came through, attendance was closer to 100 people.

There are also factors a promoter can't control. Bad weather, vans breaking down while the band is on tour, and local members of a scene traveling during the summer are just three of many reasons that a show might not do well. "We still flyer. We do a Facebook event for every show. I guess those things are effective, but it's unclear to me since we have Facebook events where people say they are going to show up, and......For me having a flyer is a visual reminder but I haven't been convinced that one is better than another," Jeremy says to me about Flywheel events. "You know, there are some shows where there's barely any promotion and 80 people show up."

Although I think RD is being shortsighted when it comes to this issue of only booking bands that a promoter likes, the larger argument advanced in the *MRR* guest column makes sense. The nuances of the argument's support are probably aligned with the thinking of many people who book shows in that promoters should feel a responsibility to do the best they can for a band and for a show.

DIY promoters book shows because they want to help their local scenes. As Mike Swiatlowski told me about booking the Old Store and the Shed in Palmer, Massachusetts, "To me the magic has always been about putting on shows in places you wouldn't expect. I never pursued or thought I should pursue booking shows at a club just because I know how to book shows. I'd rather have a regular job and just do this as a side thing and make sure that these spaces keep existing." There is an understanding that most shows will run on some type of donation basis—in part because most cities have ordinances that require a variety of licenses if a show has a ticket price. These donations tend to fall in the $5 to $10 range, depending on the number of touring bands. Good promoters either provide a meal and a place for the band to sleep or make arrangements with friends or people in the scene to host the band. There are certainly times when a DIY band or members of a band act like rock stars, but every show promoter I interviewed told me that such experiences are extremely rare. Most bands embody the alternative community spirit that is central to doing DIY. This focus on community is extended to interactions among people in a local scene and the touring bands travel mostly for the experience of playing music in new places and meeting new people. Money is not the primary motivating factor.

Claims advanced by RD and Ian MacKaye that promoters should set aside money for future shows, both offer an alternative economic model of DIY show promotion that can create a buffer for shows with low attendance. They are advocating a way of doing business that simultaneously supports individual bands and the collective good. It's ironic that the move to avoid guarantees (a mainstream touring practice deeply linked with music as capitalist product) reinforces another core feature of capitalism (each person—or in this case, band—generates her or his own income and isn't really responsible for trying to foster some type of collective income).

The general belief among promoters whom I interviewed and among punks who want to have a say in the economies of their scenes (as expressed via social media and message boards) is that the touring band should be paid based on the draw with some money going to the local bands when possible. Although the term "headliner" is almost entirely absent from DIY punk show discourse other than as a concept to critique, the touring band is treated like a headliner from an economic standpoint. Bands that don't draw won't get paid. In effect, survival of the fittest is the norm, which is no different from the capitalist contexts that guide mainstream music production and consumption. If the touring band is relying on a few streaming songs on social media sites and their demo tape or 7" isn't ready prior to the tour (the people haven't heard the tape prior to the band's arriving into town), and if the band does not feature members

of former bands that toured in the past or had some reputation, then the booker needs to have a lot of things go right for the show to do well. He or she has to hope that people will appear because they want to see some bands that night, local punks know that the person booking the show usually books good bands, or because the local bands are going to draw enough people to help the touring band make money. If the person booking the shows uses a guarantee then she or he can do as Ian MacKaye suggests: put any money beyond the guarantee aside for a day when six people show up and the touring band is looking at a $30 pay-day.

A band might draw a large crowd in a specific city, which leads to good pay; however, unless the band is really well known, success in one city does not insure that the same level of support will come to pass at the next show or series of shows. And even some of punk's best-known bands will have nights when not many people come out. Given the fluctuating attendances across cities, the band benefits from bigger paydays in some places, which helps make up for shows with poor attendances. In Chicago, for example, this general claim that our city can really help some bands for multiple days is often shared on message boards when alternative economic models are put forth (e.g., setting aside money to help start a volunteer-run community space or setting aside money to purchase a new

PA). Taking money out of a specific night's pool, might help other bands when they come to town and don't draw, but what about the band that draws here and then plays a town with a small scene or plays a show booked by a promoter in another city who doesn't collect money at the door? In this model, one scene helps make up for other scenes versus having one band make up for other bands in the same scene. The problem related to all of this back and forth about holding money or paying the full amount is that many punks who are so adamant about how punk should be pure, or free from all of capitalism's tentacles, ignore some of the struggles bands face.

Like clockwork, *MRR* is good for at least one debate a year about punk economy. Often the fireworks begin when someone writes a guest column that either claims that too many punks are too focused on making money rather than being punk or calls out the punk purists for a naïve assessment of punk. In either instance, the following issue or two of the magazine is filled with letters advocating a view that is in direct opposition to that which was advanced in the original column. These debates aren't radically different from those we see on mainstream news pundit shows, where all issues are filtered through dichotomies, limiting how people can assess the issues.

Kristen from Naked Aggression says in a January 1997 *MRR* interview that touring is "a blast!" but tempers this claim with a summary of some ways that the experience is affected by the economy of touring. "We drive anywhere from five to ten long hours every day, following the not so accurate directions to the venue, then load in our heavy equipment, set up the records and T-shirts to sell and we're stuck behind the table for three hours until we play. Then we try to find a trustworthy stranger to watch the 'merchandise' while we play, which is hard to find." Next the band works out payment and hopes there is a place to stay before starting the process again.

Phil from Naked Aggression adds another complicated feature of touring: "It's difficult when we go on a six week tour and come home broke and need to pay the rent in two weeks. And I can't really get a good job because we'll be going on tour in another month." He usually takes on construction jobs in LA, "which is really shitty because all I do is carry heavy shit around

in 100 degree heat. But I like touring so much it's worth it."

Felix Havoc writes in his January 2005 *MRR* column about his experiences booking U.S. tours for international bands. "One thing I've found in booking tours is the large gap between what bands are expected to be willing to do and what the scene is willing to provide," writes Felix. "It's one thing for a band of eighteen-year old kids with nothing to lose to throw their amps in a borrowed van and hit the road playing basement house parties for gas money. It's another thing altogether to get a band of musicians pushing 30 to fly from Europe or Japan and leave their jobs, families, and other pursuits to play basement house parties for gas money." He adds that it's harder to get these bands to commit six to eight weeks to tour the U.S. and Canada, which he would like given the requests that come to him for shows. Usually the bands have three or four weeks, but he understands why some bands aren't willing to tour the U.S. for longer periods of time. "[I]f people insist that shows should not be more than $5 and bands do not get paid more than gas money, where is the incentive for the bands to take months out of their lives to travel to places to play for less money than it costs to get there? For fun, of course, for the sake of music, of course, but if you do that for ten years or more, you get pretty tapped out for giving over huge chunks of your life to eat gas station food and sleep on floors to play for ten people and get paid less than it will cost you to get 50 miles down the road." Havoc seems to hear the cries from the purists as he writes, noting that he is not "offering a justification for bands to sell out. I am saying that without structural changes to DIY hardcore, it shouldn't be a surprise when bands break up, or leave the scene for larger labels. For a band to quit their jobs and buy gear and a van and concentrate on making quality records and play all the places that people want to see them, takes time and money."

Unfortunately, talk about money must always be couched in not losing money or show donations covering gas money rather than how punks can make a living doing punk. Again, the all-too-common sentiment is that bands that can make a living are sellouts or are driven by profit. This is ridiculous. Punks should be working to create scenes where bands, zinemakers, promoters, and label owners can earn a living in punk. Why should band members have to work full time generating profit for a restaurant owner, a bar, or a corporate retail outlet (among other low-paying jobs), but then turn around and treat punk as a money-losing hobby? Few bands have found this balance over the years, but when they do, smart punks are quick to praise those bands. "Jawbreaker are not going to be suckered into a no-win situation with a club that's going to stiff them or a kid promoter with twisted D.I.Y. ethics who thinks that anything above gas money is immoral," Ben Weasel wrote in his June 1994 *MRR* column. "They do their business by their own rules and I respect and admire them for that. Yet while every other band in

Heroin, Summer 1993, Cabbage Collective Show, Calvary Church, West Philadelphia

the country is attempting to rip off their sound, few, if any, are attempting to understand the way Jawbreaker does business, which is ultimately what gained them their popularity and probably what keeps them going."

Christian from the band Pezz focuses on the contradiction surrounding punk's economies during an interview with Jonathan Lee in *HeartattaCk* issue 35. "The whole world runs on business, exchanging money for goods and services and a lot of people are going to try to sell and buy a lot of everything. Punk rock included," Christian notes. "I mean, every DIY record label is a business—you don't give your records away and you can't produce them for free. This 'zine is a business—but it's the idea of people running their own business, bands, labels, 'zines, etc. that is a positive thing. Until they do away with capitalism we won't be able to escape it, but we can put the money back into our own hands."

Similar arguments apply to DIY spaces. Jeremy tells me, "By playing at the space you are investing in the space, keeping that option open as an alternative to showcase things you may not see at the bar or the basement because the basement's not big enough and the bar isn't going to book an experimental noise band because that's not going to sell many beers." He brings us back to the ways that individual shows can connect to a broader scene, when he adds: "[B]ig shows kind of subsidize the shows with five people at them. And that's ok."

Many promoters don't pay the local bands anything because they understand that the touring band has the greatest need. But this leaves local bands having to pay out of pocket for rehearsal spaces, to make records and tapes, to mail their music to zines and college radio stations, and to cover web costs associated with sharing their music. When local bands play for free, they are in effect underwriting their local scene. They are also subsidizing other scenes, since touring bands get to keep more of the door money, helping them get to their next show in the next town. Jordan Brand tells me, though, that the number one lesson is to treat local bands with respect. "This might get taken out of context for some people, but touring bands can fuck off if they want to have an attitude," Jordan says. "The people you gotta care about are the local bands. Touring bands are gonna come and go, but the local bands make the scene."

Thinking about various economic models helps us consider how DIY punk is done and how collective responsibility plays out in a capitalist context, both reifying and challenging mainstream approaches to music economies. From the very beginning, DIY touring was facilitated by the willingness of punks to help one another. This larger sense of sharing information for the greater good influenced one of the most important early tools to facilitate DIY touring: *Book Your Own Fuckin' Life* (*BYOFL*). *BYOFL* was tied to a more far-reaching effort to re-imagine the DIY punk show experience as something communal. In effect, *BYOFL* was the punk's booking agent, but didn't require a cut.

The first issue of *BYOFL* was released in 1992. Co-produced by *MRR* and *Profane Existence*, *BYOFL* was an early response to a growing sense that punk bands could move beyond their local scenes and punks could travel around the country and connect with one another. *BYOFL* was a more expansive extension of the "Book Your Own Fuckin' Tour" columns that *MRR* published prior to *BYOFL*. Both, however, seemed to function as more organized counterparts to the informal connections that were occurring through the personal ads in *MRR*. These personal ads were filled with requests from punks around the world looking for people with whom music could be exchanged and requests for pen pals to exchange letters about local scenes.

"I had been pen palin' everybody through *Maximum RocknRoll*," Dan Dittmer tells me. Dan, who went on to book shows in South Dakota, started a zine in 1985 when he was a teen growing up in Southern California. His correspondences with *MRR* pen pals helped Dan meet bands in other parts of the country and led to interviews for his zine as well as new friendships. A year or two later Dan was sixteen years old and decided to book a show at the Red Barn in Santa Barbara, California. He went to high school with many of the punks who were in the Nardcore scene (Oxnard, California and the surrounding cities) and met other local punks through skating sessions. When Dan told them he was going to organize the show, Nardcore punks were quick to put him in touch with bands that wanted more opportunities to play. "And I was doing this zine, so a couple of those guys that

I interviewed would say, 'I got a buddy from Santa Cruz or Santa Maria or Chula Vista or wherever who wouldn't mind jumping on the bill.' It just spread like wildfire." Twelve bands ultimately ended up on the bill. Because the Red Barn charged $100 to rent the space, Dan decided that the best way to maximize his money was to run an all day show, which started at 10:00 a.m. and ended at 10:00 p.m. "I was like, 'Fuck it, I'll take the loss [because the show was free],' but I met a shit ton of people and it worked out well that way. I was gettin' my feet wet."

He says that Santa Barbara did not have many options for punks, although there were a lot of kids hungry for the opportunity to see DIY bands. "Goldenvoice was doing shows in LA and you knew you were getting English Dogs and JFA, Angry Samoans, MDC, and that kind of stuff. And that's cool. But we're more grassroots: this guy knows a guy and we did it that way, which was awesome." Dan wrote letters to prospective bands, got phone numbers for friends of friends, and quickly discovered that there "was a crazy, weird network that had started."

Dan's combination of local relationships and national connections facilitated through the *MRR* personal ads to make this show happen in Santa Barbara reflected a common approach among people who wanted to book touring bands or who were in bands hoping to play regional shows outside their local scenes. About five years after Dan organized this show in Santa Barbra, Terry Taylor started booking shows halfway across the country in Sioux Falls, South Dakota. Terry was fifteen years old and playing in a band called Face of Decline. "The other guys in Face of Decline were eighteen to twenty years old; they were quite a bit older than me. I was little more exuberant, a little more social, talking to everybody." Terry's outgoing personality helped him connect with members of touring bands, many from the East Bay, who would then leave South Dakota and spread the word about show opportunities in Sioux Falls. "They just went around the country like everyone used to, but started giving people my number and saying I booked shows even though I had never really booked shows." The calls and letters from bands quickly followed. Terry was not alone. Punks who booked shows in other towns experienced something similar as bands were beginning to realize that the ingenuity that drove local show production could be extended out.

As show promotion became more organized, so did the tools that could facilitate DIY networking. Early word-of-mouth connections shifted slightly when Kamala Parks "compiled this large book. By state. All the promoters in every city. She would photocopy this and it got passed around all over the country. And all the bands were working off this same circuit of a promoting book," Terry tells me. "It was pre-*MRR* doing *Book Your Own Fuckin' Life*; it was the precursor to that. Those would be passed around and my name got added in there and bands were just bookin' it themselves."

Kamala (inspiration for Screeching Weasel's song, "Kamala's Too Nice") booked tours for Bay Area bands in addition to playing in Crimpshrine and Naked Aggression (among others). She saw the need to link bands and promoters so various individual efforts could develop into collective endeavors. Lenny from Filth noted in a June 1999 *MRR* interview with Karin and Lance that Kamala had helped the band plan a U.S. tour even though Filth only had one compilation track, a demo, and a 7" on the way. "[S]he gave us all the numbers and all the fuckin' free advice and a nice dinner to boot," says Lenny. As Terry mentions, *BYOFL* was the next step, a more formalized and accessible extension of Kamala's booklet that also included other types of spaces and organizations that punks should know (e.g., vegetarian restaurants, record stores, places to dumpster food). *BYOFL* became the most important tool for punk touring at that time, representing a shadow map (to borrow Stephen Duncombe's phrase used in *Notes from Underground*) of the U.S. And at a meta-level, the resources presented in *BYOFL*, like Kamala's guide, let readers know what could be developed if punks were willing to try to make things happen (i.e., the explicit and implicit focus of DIY on the "You can do this, too" was embodied in this zine).

This sentiment is explicitly reflected in Jason Mojica's introduction to the third issue of *BYOFL*, which was released in 1994. "We could quit all of this and just work, eat, and watch TV like everyone else. And a lot of people will, half the things listed in here will probably vanish within a few years," claims Mojica.

"But a lot won't...why? What drives so many people to work their asses off, to the extent of becoming total maniacs, in this wacky world we call punk? Satisfaction, belonging, 'fame', the desire to escape ordinary life, and just plain fun are a few of the reasons, but it all comes down to love. We love what we are doing, or at least we should. If you don't love what you're doing, then maybe you shouldn't be doing it at all. But for the lovers...here's a bunch of others who feel the same way as you. Write 'em, call 'em, play with 'em, record 'em, and sleep in their houses. But be nice! These people don't want to be shit on anymore than you do."

Dan Dittmer notes that it took time to distinguish the flakes from people who were doing good work. Once he was able to make these distinctions, Dan then re-focused his attention on the byproducts of *BYOFL* and the culture that was being enacted through the zine. "I loved it because half these bands weren't JFAs, Angry Samoans, and all that kind of stuff," he says to me. "[Y]ou were going to do a garage party or whatever and then you started seeing these kids who don't have to pay $11 and could only pay $3 and still have a good time. Back in the day I remember paying $11 to see Butthole Surfers and Uniform Choice in Oxnard. I was like, 'Wow, that's a lot of money,' especially being a young teen."

Al ("Pist") Ouimet tells me that The Pist formed at the beginning of 1993 and went on their first tour that summer. "We did the whole U.S. in six weeks; it was six weeks and thirteen shows. So we had a lot of downtime. It was done almost entirely through *Book York Own Fucking Life*. That was the resource back then, pre-Internet," says Al. "That was the reference guide for doing anything like that: mailing out demo tapes and 7"s and whatever we had. We got whatever shows we could and tried to get more as we went. Some canceled along the way and others popped up here and there." When the band returned to Connecticut at the end of the tour, they immediately looked to rent a house where they could practice, but also where they could book bands. This is how *BYOFL* implicitly contributed to the growth of a national scene: bands learned that the zine could be a guide to book shows, they toured and experienced the difference between DIY shows in their scenes and in other scenes, including the nuances that distinguish amazing experiences, shows, and spaces from those that were average or very poor.

Chris Moore, who now drums for Coke Bust and Sick Fix, tells me that his experience was very similar to what happened with The Pist. Chris and fellow Magrudergrind members were in high school. They didn't know anyone who had toured before so they couldn't lean on friends in the Washington, DC scene for advice. "But we got our hands on that zine *Book Your Own Fuckin' Life* and we booked the whole tour from that zine," he tells me. "Our plan was to do two weeks, but because we were fifteen, our parents didn't want us to leave the house for two weeks. So we did one week in the Northeast and came home for a few days. Then we did another week. Most of the shows sucked, but I made some friends on that tour that I am still friends with now."

The touring bands created links by communicating information about show spaces and promoters to one another and sharing stories about different scenes. "What was cool about these bands is that all these kids were probably thinking: 'I'm in the middle of Nevada and I have nothing to do.' Or 'I'm in the middle of Idaho," Dan tells me. "And 'We've got two bands and you've got three bands. I like your band and you like my band.' People would exchange tapes or whatever. And most of the promoters were in bands so they knew both sides of the bill." Bull Gervasi shares a similar sentiment with me, describing how something

UNIVERSAL ORDER OF ARMAGEDDON (md)

ASKANCE (va)

POLICY OF THREE (nj)

Saturday, April 24th
2:00 PM matinee
Mt. Lodge #6
34th & M streets
(Georgetown, N.W. Washington D.C.)
$5 / all ages
(more info, call 703-908-9347)

TO THE PARENT
Start your child on a voyage of discovery into the world of knowledge through these fun punk rock concerts. Children develop many important skills through the art of dancing, and these skills—eye-hand coordination, color concepts and picture comprehension—form the foundation for early learning success. Remember, children who dance acquire and use knowledge more efficiently and effectively!

new seemed to come together for punks in the early '90s. "It was the early stages of that scene in '93 so there were folks like us doing shows in Philly who were trying to do shows in their towns and some of the bands that we had become friendly with through booking shows or writing to, kind of hooked us up in some of the cities we played in [during Policy of Three's first tour of the U.S. in summer 1993]."

In 1996 *MRR* worked with the Philadelphia-based Bleeding Heart Collective to produce issue 5 of *BYOFL*. The collective notes in the introduction to this issue that *BYOFL* is in effect a marker laid down on behalf of a DIY spirit in a culture that is flooded with a range of corporate options. "Massive mergers create even larger media giants deciding what we're told. A fifteen-year-old makes ten new friends around the country with a hand-colored comic she drew in detention. A popular local bookstore is forced out of business by a new chain store with the multinational backing to do it. Three friends start a volunteer-run record store with an emphasis on 'bands we like.' This week's popular band plays their MTV hit to 10,000 strangers in a poorly attended stadium show. Some band you've never heard of plays their guts out in your packed basement for you and your twenty friends."

BYOFL would eventually shift from a paper zine to an online guide, although the mix of engaged participants and flakes continued. Nicole Pagowsky tells me that when she was booking shows at two different houses in Madison, Wisconsin she remembers "actually responding to some bands and they would be like, 'Thank you for replying; I've contacted a bunch of people through this *Book Your Own Fuckin' Life* site and you're one of the only people that responded.'" The site is now basically dormant. Others picked up the slack: Do DIY, local websites run by community spaces or infoshops, Tumblr sites focused on specific scenes, and Facebook groups.

Terry Taylor says that his early shows were mostly coordinated via the mail rather than through phone calls. The tools people can use to coordinate shows now are vastly superior: domestic mobile phone calling plans, texting, email, social media instant messaging programs, and international calling via a variety of Internet programs are all very cheap and sometimes free. The loss of intimacy that came with receiving letters and band demos via the mail or calls from people throughout the country is traded out for increased efficiency and radical reduction in cost. Prior to telecommunication deregulation in 1996 and the emergence of a cellular phone marketplace, long distance calls were extremely expensive. This meant that someone like Terry, who was a teenager and living at home when he started doing shows, was not going to be making long-distance calls to coordinate shows. This context of phone calls is important not only because we can understand how difficult it was to coordinate compared to contemporary times—but also because it is interesting to consider how a fifteen-year-old kid in South Dakota was able to become a go-to person for shows in that part of the country. And he was not alone, since other kids in other parts of the country were booking touring bands.

Chances are that many contemporary promoters won't know that punks in the past were dodging cops to keep shows going, creatively using any kind of space they could find to do shows, negotiating the extreme hatred of punk expressed by mainstream institutions, and creating publications that could foster regional and national networks. But the kids who started booking shows in the mid-to-late 1990s into the present have figured out ways to keep money in their scenes and foster places where punk politics and culture are spatially enacted. Two of the most important developments that began in the 1990s, and continue to thrive today, are the staging of house shows and the establishment of volunteer-run community spaces. Both materialize DIY in important ways, but each has a unique historical trajectory.

Section III

Caught Dreaming

Doc Hopper, 4/21/94 - Philadelphia, House Show

The Kids are United

We all probably have embarrassing experiences that we can share. And these incidents exist on a spectrum: "Hey, you'll never believe this stupid thing I just did..." to the more extreme, where even thinking about the encounter might call forth a flood of shameful emotions. One of the moments that stands out for me occurred when I was twelve years old. My friend Ron and I agreed that I would go to his house after we both finished eating dinner. As I approached the driveway, I shouted up to him. His bedroom was in the front of the house on the second floor of a two-story suburban tract home. I walked up the steps that led to his front door. I was lost in my thoughts, reflecting on whatever foolishness would have been rattling around my pre-teen head. I opened the front door and walked into his house. His mom and stepdad were in the kitchen, which was about fifteen feet straight ahead from the front door.

"What are you doing?!" Ron's step-dad asked with an exasperated tone.

"Um, when I was walking up the driveway, Ron said I should just come in," I stuttered through the lie.

"You don't walk into people's homes," he said, emphasizing the word "don't." I stared at him with a dumb look on my face and hoped this one-way conversation would end quickly. Time seemed to pass at an excruciatingly slow speed. Finally he said, "Go on up."

When I reached Ron's room, he asked me what that was all about. I explained that I spaced out and just walked into the house. Ron laughed at me, but before the true teasing could begin he was called downstairs to be yelled at by his parents for letting his friend walk in the door without knocking first.

There are a variety of basic social codes people follow during daily life: observing appropriate spatial distances from one another based on context, walking to the back of a line and waiting if people are queuing for some reason (e.g., to purchase items at a grocery store or to withdraw money from an ATM), answering the phone with some kind of greeting, and refraining from walking into people's houses unless granted permission to enter. But if we think about the examples that aren't walking into another person's home, cutting in line (accidentally) or standing too close to someone—perhaps in an elevator or on a bus after crowds thin but not noticing the thinning—would not be a form of embarrassment most of us would remember a few minutes later, and certainly not decades later.

Yeah, I felt bad because I did something stupid and was judged negatively by my friend's parents. At the same time, I was a kid, and kids do a lot of thoughtless things. As I aged, though, I began to understand more fully what it meant to enter someone's house without a direct invitation. I developed a greater awareness of the home as the ultimate private space: a site of

Lemuria, 06/05/10, Fucking Discovery Zone, New Haven, CT

safety, familiarity, and comfort. Setting aside more complicated and important arguments about the range of social, political, and economic problems that surround private property, where one dwells is very much a symbolic and material extension of one's being. We imbue where we live with some sense of ourselves even through minor decisions, such as choosing colors to paint the walls, selecting furniture, and organizing the space. And we expect that the home can be a protected domain in which we have some control.

Public policy scholar Robert Putnam garnered widespread attention for his book *Bowling Alone*. Putnam explores the function of social capital, or networks of trust, in contemporary and historical public life. The title of the book references one of the key examples used to illustrate shifts in public interactions: bowling in the U.S. has increased but enrollments in bowling leagues have decreased, which means people choose forms of entertainment and activities that they can do with a small group of friends or family rather than with strangers.

This larger argument about social isolation finds a spatial complement in Ray Oldenburg's *The Great Good Place*. Oldenburg claims that there is a dearth of informal spaces of social interaction in the U.S., spaces that he calls "third places". These third places, which thrive in Europe and Latin America, include cafes, pubs, and marketplaces. He contends that people in the U.S. tend to focus on the "first place" (home) or the "second place" (work) for social interaction over and against the third places. Although cafes have proliferated since Oldenburg's book was published in 1991, such spaces tend be littered with earbud-wearing laptop users who exist in the presence of others but are isolated in their own personal technological bubbles.

Oldenburg argues that people in the U.S. have turned further inward to the comforts and familiarity of the home where interactions can be controlled and the people with whom one engages can be carefully screened. Individuals can then weed out and better avoid people who are not family or friends. Although the arguments advanced by Putnam, Oldenburg, and others, make a lot of sense, I think there are alternative ways to consider the home and social life. There are some cracks and gaps in the more common conceptions of the home as a somewhat

isolated private sphere. The emergence of the house as a DIY venue explicitly and implicitly challenges conceptions of the home as cut off from public life. Houses are transformed from somewhat isolated private spheres to pseudo-public spaces when punks decide to host shows in their homes. House show spaces are now standard locations for punk shows and are considered important options for DIY punk bands touring the U.S.; however, this contemporary awareness among punks that houses can function as venues did not develop uniformly. The contemporary DIY touring network is very much a product of efforts made in the 1980s but shifted and changed throughout the 1990s because of some limitations with the more common spaces used for shows during the '80s.

Punk bands have played at houses since the music began. This history is not necessarily unique to punk, since domestic spaces are used to share music in various ways. Bands that practice in garages invite friends to hear music. People throw dance parties in their houses that are soundtracked by DJs. And backyard parties often feature a band or multiple bands playing covers and/or original songs of varying genres. There is, however, a major difference between these other uses of the home for collective music experiences and punk house shows. The people who live in the house and book the shows are enacting a DIY philosophy and politics, as are the bands that play and many of the people in attendance. The home space has in effect been appropriated to shift from a container for standard domestic practices to a pseudo-public place that offers an alternative venue option for many DIY punk bands that are often excluded from more official (or legitimate) live music venues. With that said, most early house shows were treated differently from the shows that happen today, often viewed as parties or one-off opportunities to see local bands rather than *the* destination for touring bands to play with local bands.

In the early-to-mid 1980s, for example, the fanzine *Fight For Freedom*, which covered the LA and Orange County punk scenes, regularly featured a "Gigs and Parties Reviewed" section. The January/February 1984 issue blended reviews of regular punk haunts, such as the Cathay de Grande, Roxanne's in Arcadia, Ichabods in Anaheim, and Perkins Palace in Pasadena, with a variety of houses. All of the house reviews are listed as parties, not shows. One reviewer writes: "We got off a little late to this party, but well worth the effort" in reference to "some house in Lkwd [Lakewood]" where Death Roster, Body Count, and Mortis played on November 19, 1983. "Another band Us Kids? (is that it?) was goin up when the Lkwd. cops decide to give a little visit. You all know the rest!" A second review listed under the heading of "another I.O.U. party at Bobs [sic] house Dec 16th" begins by explaining to readers that "Bob had this party cuz he was gonna do three months in juvee." Once again the night ends earlier than planned when the police arrive. The band I.O.U. (Impact on Youth) "pulled off two sets that got a few people slamming, but at around 11:00 the O.C. Pigz busted it up." Seven years later we find a nearly identical story told by Joey Discrepancy in a February 1991 *MRR* scene report about Northern California. Joey writes that there are very few places for bands to play in San Jose other than a pizza place. "Some cool people with a huge yard and an old barn have also hosted some festive punk-type gatherings." He highlights a Fourth of July party, noting that the last band was not able to play because the show was "cut off by the bullies in blue."

One key distinction between these parties from the past and the house shows that happen now is some general relationships among people in the space. That is, when one attended a party, one might not know everyone at that party, but more than likely most people in attendance were familiar to one another because

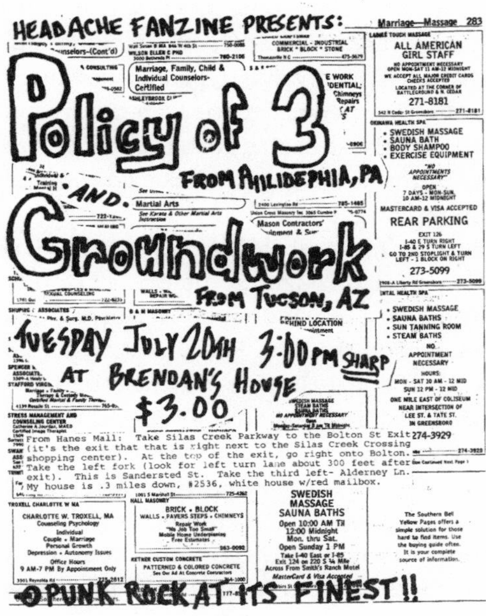

the scenes were so much smaller then. The parties were not radically different from any other party in that people who moved in similar social circles gathered together to hang out. More contemporary house shows, on the other hand, can have a much more diverse and fluctuating collection of people in attendance.

Kim Nolan, who was involved with some of the first shows at the Fireside Bowl in Chicago and an active member of Chicago's various scenes in the 1980s and 1990s, tells me about her experiences attending shows on the South Side of Chicago in the mid-to-late 1980s when she was in middle school and high school. "I would say that the basement shows would be a place where I would know everybody after a while, whereas the VFW Hall was a lot bigger. I don't want to say those were huge shows, but they were a lot bigger, maybe 200 people. But I didn't necessarily know everybody." She adds that shows at the VFW Hall always felt different compared to the basement shows, mostly because "it would be bands that came from other parts of the city" even though the bands weren't well-known outside Chicago. "And at the basement shows it was a Friday night party that people were going to play at." These bands were regulars at the house shows and tended to be hyperlocal support at the VFW shows.

There are some exceptions to this early use of the house for a party, although sporadic, where punks instead understood that houses could function as recurring venues for shows. I am reminded of a scene report in the May/June 1985 issue of *MRR*. "Right now the problem is that the underground clubs and houses have been closed down mainly due to people moving or getting evicted," writes Mimi in reference to the Eugene, Oregon scene. "For the most part, the places to play are basements (very rare)" and then she lists University of Oregon followed by some clubs as more consistent options.

Many of the spaces used for local DIY shows in the 1980s have remained options in cities throughout the U.S. since that time: VFW Halls, skate parks, community youth centers, and city parks. Bull Gervasi booked the first Policy of 3 tour that happened in the summer of 1993. He tells me that the band only played all-ages spaces, adding that "the VFW Hall type of space maybe dominated a bit more. I think in that time period that those types of spaces (the Elks Lodge or whatever) were a popular one for punks to do shows and were more successful than other types of spaces." In theory, these spaces reflect the kind of third places that various critics would like to see thrive in the U.S., sites where people can enact a vibrant and engaged local public life. However, amidst many successes booking punk shows in these types of community spaces one also finds a range of recurring problems.

First, punk has historically maintained a reputation for being destructive and that status seems to lurk like some sort of phantom menace even when shows run smoothly. The harsh sounds don't make sense to most of the people responsible for renting public and community spaces and these managers are perhaps operating with a stereotypical image of punks: charged hair and safety pins through their noses, spitting at one another. If there are any problems at a show, people in charge are quick to stop renting to punk promoters. Problems at a birthday celebration will likely be viewed as an anomaly, whereas something going wrong at—a punk show, for example—will be considered the norm. Second, the rental fee, which might not include a PA system (or a person to run sound), can take money out of the scene. The funds required to rent a space could have been used to pay touring bands or to raise money for an organization through a benefit show. Finally, the likelihood that a show promoter might have to dip into her or his pockets

to cover expenses if the show does not draw enough people increases since rental fees must be paid. These issues are not unique to a specific region or time period and are regularly featured in stories told to me by punks who shifted away from booking these types of spaces to booking house shows.

Josh Otten helped start the FSU Garage, a house space in Cedar Falls, Iowa. He grew up in Marshalltown, Iowa, which is a small factory town about an hour from Des Moines (and perhaps best known as the title of a Modern Life is War record). "The first shows I went to were actually DIY shows. These kids who were a bit older and around town wanted to play" so they booked shows that featured other Iowa bands in an effort to create something bigger that would attract more local kids. This was around 1996 and the kids were booking the Coliseum, which is a typical city community center; it contains a gymnasium, some large and small rooms, and city offices. Josh tells me that the room where the bands played held about 200 people and had a small stage, which was perfect for their shows. The rent was $100. "I remember that somebody who worked for the building would be there to make sure kids don't go in places they're not supposed to, because it was a big place. They would be there, but we were always very respectful and tried to be very respectful

Universal Order of Armageddon, Summer 1993, Cabbage Collective Show, Calvary Church, West Philadelphia

because that sort of authority figure, you don't want somebody to shut down this good thing that you have."

Josh, like so many punks who book shows, quickly moved from simply being in attendance when bands played to being involved with organizing the shows. Although Josh and his friends did not encounter problems with the city employees responsible for renting the Coliseum, the rental fees were too high. They decided to move everything to a local city park, which was much cheaper (around $30). But once expenses were down, problems with the city started to emerge. "At first we would tell them we were doing shows and bunch of people were playing, and then people would get upset that you were charging. So then we would say we were taking donations, mandatory donations," Josh remembers. "It eventually got to a point that whoever in the parks and rec wasn't too keen on what we were doing. You attract a couple hundred kids to an area and something's going to go down. They started to get a little more strict with renting it out and it got more and more difficult in Marshalltown to throw these DIY shows."

This concern that "something's going to go down" referenced fears among city officials about fights, underage drinking, or some perceived drug use. Josh says that none of these problems were prevalent. In the very rare situation when a fight would happen, things were worked out among the people at the show. And given the presence of an active straight edge movement, the few kids who wanted to drink would go to their cars rather than drink in the park. Therefore, the pressure on Josh's crew was really about a city employee not believing that punk could be positive, and likely upset by the loud, fast noise.

Mike Swiatlowski, who would go on to create a DIY spaced called Old Store and helped book another called The Shed, also experienced this close-minded roadblock when he was helping coordinate one of his first shows in Palmer, Massachusetts in the late 1990s. Mike and his friends started by lining up a local band called Super Agent that was made up of other friends from the scene. "But then word spread and we got requests from like ten bands," recalls Mike. He was shocked that there was so much interest. This flood of interest can be very surprising for someone who has no idea how to do a show and assumes that even small punk bands have multiple and better alternatives than playing a show for someone without a track record. As Jen Angel writes in the December 1994 issue of *MRR* (the second of a three part series about putting on shows), "It's not hard to get bands to play." She notes that many bands will play for free if one just asks and is nice, but the context of her comment is someone doing a show for the first time and likely booking a space that will cost money, which can cut into opportunities to pay bands. In some sense, efforts by individuals without promotion experience are tests to see if DIY is real, opportunities to witness if the thing they believe in a is a fairytale or only true for punks who live in other cities and towns. "We ended up having five bands on that first show. We booked the American Legion Hall in Palmer. We said we'd have music play, they said sure, we were all set with the date, and I made flyers," Mike explains. "Just as we started handing out flyers, word started to spread around town about what we were doing because it had never really been done before. People started to freak out and someone told the Legion that it was gonna be a bunch of kids and they're gonna break everything, which was so not us. They called and said, 'This thing's canceled' without giving me any explanation about it. I was furious and totally broken."

Nevin Marshall and his friends were also met with city restrictions at the Fort Myers Skate Park in Fort Myers, Florida in the early 2000s, although this problem developed over time.

"The lady that owned it lived in a different town so our friend ran it for her and my buddy worked there, so basically we could do whatever we wanted," he tells me. The combination of an absentee owner and a built-in audience via kids who were there to skate meant that Nevin's group of friends were able to book shows at the skate park for a few years, which is a nice timespan for these types of spaces. "Some kids would come just to skate and some would come for the show. It really helped the bands because even if you didn't get a turnout for the show, all the people that came to skate. Everyone paid $5 on the way in, so the bands would do ok," Nevin remembers. "Even if it was a Tuesday night and not that many people came out for the show, you could be confident to get them a decent amount of gas money." Fort Myers is a smaller city, not a top destination like Jacksonville, Tampa, or Miami, and is located in a state that already was and remains a more difficult destination for touring bands given the length of time it takes to dip down into Florida. If anything was going to happen in a city like Fort Myers, the punks had to do it themselves—and they needed to be resourceful.

But inventiveness only takes one so far when faced with a more bureaucratic ownership. The city bought the space, and everything changed. "I'm not exactly sure what happened, but the guy that we knew was always down for it but then there was a guy who was more of a city employee and we couldn't... It was all sort of under the radar there. As obvious as it was, the people running this thing were absentee but once the city had more of a presence we couldn't really do it anymore."

Nevin points to an important shift in the space itself relative to city control, but when he remarks that he is not sure what happened, he is playing with time in an interesting way. That is, speaking from the standpoint of his late teens/early twenties he might not have fully understood why the city wasn't supporting uses of the space that extended beyond, but linked to, skateboarding. However, Nevin is now older and much more experienced with DIY punk shows. He has toured domestically and internationally and has booked house shows in Fort Myers since the skate park stopped doing shows. Therefore, he certainly understands what happened to the skate park once the city was in charge.

Putting all of one's efforts into creating something special only to have those endeavors undermined can be disheartening and frustrating. The highs are monumental when punk shows go well, and the lows are extreme when plans come undone (especially for young punks just starting to book bands). David Ensminger speaks to this general point when he describes the emotional experiences tied to finding a scene early in one's punk life. "When you're sixteen or seventeen, you think, 'This is it; it doesn't get any better than this,'" he tells me. "Because you don't go to bars, you don't understand how they operate. And once you actually do get of age, and do go to the bars, you're kind of disappointed because it doesn't have that original flair. It doesn't have everything else that is being offered; it's sort of all business."

There is this strange combination of total awareness and total naiveté when it comes to doing one's first DIY shows. In each of these examples—Josh in Marshalltown, Mike in Palmer, and Nevin in Fort Myers—teenagers and people in their early twenties knew that they did not have access to punk shows. Either the bands weren't coming to their towns or the bands were playing bars with age limits, which would prohibit these kids from seeing the shows. Therefore, these guys were completely aware of the context in which they were working relative to seeing punk bands. But then there is often a lack of understanding when it comes to a political economy of music, which is expressed when David notes that seeing the other side of music through the lens of a more formalized and official music industry highlights how liberating the DIY experience can be. When I was interviewing people for this book, there was a palpable difference between descriptions of people's first efforts to book shows and their experiences later on. Accounts of early shows were told with an "I can't believe we pulled it off" tone. They felt a surge in the beginning and fed off the energy, but over time, while they remained motivated by the community aspects or continued to understand that their efforts are needed, they lost that sense of awe.

If city and community spaces come with a variety of problems related to control and cost, the house presents a polar opposite option. The use of one's house for shows is ideal for many punks because rent covers a place to live, and having the space for shows is a bonus. There is no need to deal with city employees worried that punks will fuck up the space when doing shows in one's house; no need to deal with store owners who back out at the last minute because of concerns with the primary business (often food) since punk shows are usually just treated as extra income; or with fire marshals or local political figures to approve permits. Instead, the house appears to offer a very simple option (in theory): a space where people can gather who want to see bands and an opportunity to keep money in the scene.

If we think about the quality of public life, it's ironic that the home can be a more public-focused alternative to the potentially limited and limiting community-based spaces. The community halls and city parks are public spaces, but as sites of public life these places are not always able to cater equally to all members of a town or city. Calling out a variety of people who don't understand punk is not really breaking news for many punks, who often struggle to do what they want amidst pressures to "be normal" or adopt more mainstream values. But other punks, especially young punks, might be less versed in the rules that are created and enforced by adults with authority. The stories told by Jeff, Mike, and Nevin feature similar narrative arcs. Each tried to work within the context of more formal community-based spaces, but each was let down because the people in charge of

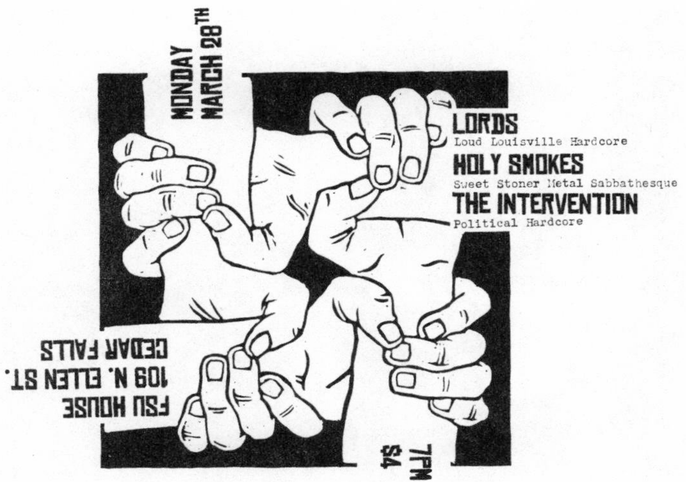

those spaces consider punk to be unimportant or a nuisance. But these three guys, like so many other men and women, young and old, who book punk shows in the U.S., continued to search for alternatives because they understood the importance of live music and that opportunities for punks to get together in a show space is crucial for a scene to develop and be sustained.

The daydreamer who wanders into a house without knocking is a less politicized version of the kid who is unaware that houses are not supposed to be show spaces. Both enter into spaces without approval. My entry into Ron's house was merely a product of stupidity, whereas punks involved with house shows have directly challenged established mainstream music industry norms for touring and show promotion. The gatekeepers who think they are supposed to make decisions about who gets to play and when (and then suck away the profits) are discarded. Some punks are well aware of this, and others develop an understanding of the cultural politics after some time has passed.

"I didn't know that house shows existed when I did the first house show on October 14, 1995," Alexander Lescher says to me. "I had no idea that anyone else had ever done a house show." Alexander grew up about 55 miles northwest of Philadelphia in Reading, Pennsylvania. He was interested in metal and then

Parasol MA, 04/28/12, Flywheeel, Easthampton, MA

discovered heavier punk bands through more cutting edge columns in metal magazines. Alexander soon started attending all-ages shows at a local venue but had not been exposed to DIY promotion through people in this scene or through the publications he was reading at that time. That first show he did in 1995 happened in the living room of his father's house. "It was rather comedic because I was running around the whole time, taking pictures. It was like an '80s movie where somebody is throwing a party and their parents don't know about it." Although Alexander did not start with community spaces, he was motivated by the same factors that many DIY promoters consider. That is, he did the show in his home "because it was a space and it was free." Alexander soon learned that he was not alone when it came to organizing house shows. "A few weeks later, maybe *HeartattaCk* 8 or something like that came out and I started reading more about house shows and then read about classic Bad Brains shows in houses in DC."

Because this first show was more chaotic than he expected, feeling a bit too much like an out-of-control party, Alexander took a break from booking shows. But the experience of doing that show was in part a way to personalize his budding interest in DIY as a philosophy that can be put into practice rather than merely existing in the realm of ideals. "Basically as I got more involved in punk, I knew more people and there was this more empowering feel to it. Summer of '95 was huge for me, discovering new bands and discovering the extent of DIY and that I was able to move forward with that and be a part of it." This engagement with DIY meant that Alexander could shift from being a guy who did a one-off house show to someone who was looking to contribute to something bigger. In 1997 he started doing shows again in a somewhat more organized fashion after an Internet friend in Florida asked if Alexander could book Revelation Records band Morning Again. "This time I not only had to secure everything for the show, I had to figure out how to do a show properly. I was seventeen at the time. I was not very wise. I had to have people attend the show to be able to pay this band. I had to find other bands. And those things just did not exist so readily in Reading. And also make it not apparent to my father."

If younger kids are doing shows in their homes regularly, then parents have usually agreed that the shows can happen, which is also something that would distinguish the home as a regular show space versus the house as a location for a one-off party. The latter happens when parents are out-of-town. Interestingly, some parents are eager to help out in whatever way they can. For example, Al Rios, who is one of the bookers at volunteer-run community space 1919 Hemphill in Fort Worth, Texas and is in the pop punk band Special Guest, had his first house show experiences at his parents' home. "When I was coming into it, it was kind of like in between big flourishes of activity, so there wasn't a punk club," Al tells me. "There were house shows but I was a little young for that, 'cause it was mostly parties where people were drinking and I was fourteen, a freshman in high school. I started having shows at my parents' house. It was completely different from what a house show normally is because it was real tame and my mom would make tacos." He adds that his mom was really excited that touring bands would play shows there and then spend the night. The bands would sleep in a guest room and Al's mom would make them breakfast in the morning. Al estimates that he did six or seven shows and notes that everything ran smoothly because his parents are easygoing and supportive people. "But nothing happened that would have made a reasonable person upset. It was always really polite, really good, and everyone was super-respectful."

A similar scenario is discussed in the documentary *Between Resistance and Community*, directed by Joe Caroll and Ben Holtzman. The film focuses on the DIY punk scene in Long Island, including the importance of house shows there. The Vargas House is one of the regular show spaces, but the space feels a little different because the Vargas' mom is an important presence. Jimmy from the band Shotwell notes: "Here's this family and it's not just kids saying, 'Hey mom, I'm going to have a show in the basement and there's nothing you can do about it.'" Instead, Jimmy claims Ms. Vargas provides meals for the bands and people in the scene after shows; she is central to helping make this scene vital even if she isn't booking shows or necessarily interested in the music. Jimmy's observations about Ms. Vargas reflect the ways that bands that play houses will come into contact with parents, which some band members might not have expected. "When you play random shows you know that you're going to play places where you realize that no one in this room is old enough to live in an apartment," Zack Furness tells me. "We're hoping to stay with someone's folks, which can lead to some hilarious next morning conversations over donuts: 'So you teach college?' And I'm like, 'Absolutely, ma'am.'"

Because Alexander was doing shows without his father's knowledge, he didn't want to chance that the chaos of that first show would continue and that something end up getting wrecked in the house. He started using the basement instead, which was inspiration for name of the space: The Bassmint. Alexander's father worked as a bartender, "so he would leave at 7:00 p.m. and I would be like, 'Show starts at 8:00. Don't be early.' And everyone had to be out by 2:00. Usually they were gone well before that." It's amazing that he was able to run shows so long (June 1997 until 1998) without his father finding out, but the secret was discovered when "this band Silent Majority from Long Island had a bus, like a small bus. My father came home and was like, 'Someone at the bar said there was a bus in the driveway.'"

Alexander's father ultimately responded to the shows in a way that mirrored Al's parents and the Vargas' mom, telling Alexander that bands could play as long as Alexander provided some advance notice and made sure nothing was stolen and the basement was not damaged. Alexander adds that his dad "became a huge part of it" because touring bands could now stay at the house. Moreover, because his father raced cars as a hobby, there was an excellent collection of tools at the house and his father was excited about helping bands that were constantly experiencing problems with vans. "There was a band from Germany. They got here and their van wasn't working properly so they had to take a day off from tour and he worked with them all day long. He got them back on the road..."

If one were to closely assess subject matter in punk lyrics, I am confident that anger directed at parents would be in the top twenty recurring themes. Of course, this focus on problems with one's parents is mostly linked to the quantity of punk bands formed by teenagers. Teenagers often lack the life experiences that can inspire more sophisticated lyrics and song narratives. However, Alexander's experiences highlight that for younger punks, parents can be crucial support for the development of a house show scene. This is especially true in smaller towns where all-ages alternatives are lacking.

John Boilard (aka JP Boneyard) booked shows with Mike Swiatlowskiat at The Shed in Palmer, Massachusetts from April

2000-November 2005. The Shed was literally a shed in John's backyard. The space could comfortably hold 30-35 people, but often many more people were packed into The Shed for shows. John started playing in local bands when he was fourteen or fifteen years old but he was also eager to participate in the scene beyond playing shows. He did this by helping out Mike Swiatlowski with another local storefront space called The Old Store. When that space closed, John suggested moving shows to The Shed. "Originally The Shed is where we set up to practice. My mom was used to the noise and everything," John tells me. "The concept was to invite another band to play with us and then invite some friends, which didn't seem too far out there. But she didn't realize what she was getting into when 'Now I wanna have four or five bands and they're not from town. I don't know these people; I just know their bands.' And now 100 people have showed up." Although John's mom didn't understand what it meant to turn the backyard shed into a venue, hindsight highlights that the noise and chaos were tolerated for larger reasons. "She would let me do all of these things in and around the house because she could keep an eye on me," he says. "She preferred that. 'I know he's probably gonna cause trouble but at least I can see him.'"

Many of the scenarios where kids are doing shows in the family home are single-parent households. James Payne, who grew up in suburban Ohio explains that the first show he organized happened while his mom was on a trip to China. The show featured local bands, including his own folk-punk band. Then he booked a band from Miami called Baby Calendar without a clear plan for a show space. "I don't know what I was thinking, maybe that I would have it somewhere else but then something fell through," James explains. He asked his mom to stay at a friend's house for the night so he could do the show. "It was only me and my mother at that time living in our house. I just convinced her like, 'You know, it's going to be ok, just let me do this.' And she actually agreed to it, which is absurd." He adds that his mom was always really supportive, and her willingness to let him do the show was sort of in character. James' parents divorced when he was eight years old. "I suppose you could say that my father and stepmother had a more comfortable lifestyle

and often were able to take me on posh vacations and give me gifts. My mother was mainly only able to take care of me in a less flashy, though ultimately more meaningful, way. Doing things like this—which were a big deal but not costly—was one thing she could afford to do."

Alexander, Al, John, and James learned to do shows while living at home. Doing shows at one's family home is a bit more of an anomaly when considering the bulk of house show spaces, and all four men would continue to book shows once they left their family homes.

Most house venues develop because people in their early-to-mid twenties have the autonomy (living away from one's parents), the space to do shows, and a desire to participate more fully in their local scenes by hosting bands. Some of these punks understand that if they don't do the shows, there won't be options for DIY punk in that town. Perhaps houses that were doing shows have closed, or nobody else has been able to combine interest and the ability to follow through.

Jenny Ray, who books 406 Haskell (an all-ages DIY community space in Dallas, Texas), tells me that Dallas has historically featured options for punk shows but that the spaces were constantly in flux as bar-venues opened and closed. Oddly, the lack of all-ages alternatives in Dallas and the cost that accompanied going to see bands in bars had not motivated punks to create alternative show space options. "To my knowledge, there's never been a lot of house spots in Dallas. I don't know what it is." When she moved into the Bike House with some friends, they knew they had to do shows there. "You walked in and it was one big room, there was an archway, and there was another big room. So it was just perfect to have shows in that one big long space of a room. We started having the shows and they were just ridiculous, kids always just went insane, and it was really a fun time." The Bike House was especially exciting, says Jenny, because punks in Dallas were so eager to see bands. "Sometimes it would be two or three a week." The first show happened at Bike House on February 28, 2008 but the space didn't have the run that she hoped for when they first moved into the house. "Toward the end of 2008 we had to stop and then we still had a couple shows here and there, testing our luck." Their last show was in 2009 because of pressures from the neighbors.

One of Jenny's roommates was in a band. Being in a band is often a key influence on decisions to host shows in one's house. Members of the band decide at some point that the space is not only good for band practice but also could work for shows. Some renters come to this conclusion before the lease is signed, whereas others figure out that the house will meet show space needs after living in the house for a while.

The first incarnation of Casa de Chaos in Sacramento, California was not initially considered as a show space. Mickie Rat, who has been in the band the Secretions since 1991, found

The Copyrights, 10/21/11, 25th Anniversary Show, Lost Cross House, Carbondale, IL

the house in 1992. It was sandwiched between two fraternity houses (all three had been frat houses since the 1950s). Mickie's friends needed a practice space and kicked in some money for the rent in exchange for access to the basement. "It was a dirt-floor basement in an old Victorian Craftsman-style house," Mickie informs me. "The basement actually wasn't tall enough to stand in, so they dug the basement out a little bit deeper so you could stand in it. It was nothing but river dirt. They put some carpet down and built a riser for the drums and it was a practice space." That band soon broke up, but the space was now set for other bands to practice and for Mickie to host shows from time to time.

During 1993 and 1994 shows happened often enough for Casa de Chaos to be considered a consistent DIY space. "I think the most legendary show of that time, which was in '93 or '94, was the band Fifteen," Mickie recalls. "I was out of town but my roommate wanted to do a show. There were reportedly 200-300 people at that show, packing the backyard and the basement and just going crazy." The basement holds about 40 people, but many shows would draw close to 100 people, with around 60 in the basement at any given time and the rest hanging out in the backyard. This show was obviously more intense. "I came home and there were more beer bottles than I have ever seen in my life carpeting the backyard and the basement. I thought that there was no way 200 people were there but when I got home and went into the backyard, 'Good lord, they were right.'"

Mickie moved out of the house because he was getting married, but his roommates continued to book shows for a little bit longer. By 1996 everyone moved out who was involved with shows. Five years later Mickie was getting divorced and he noticed that the house was for rent again. "I went down to the basement and everything we had built (a little practice space, a little stage, and everything) was completely torn out, so we had to build that up again. That took a couple years. I think we started doing shows there in 2004 or 2005."

In part this long run, which is not the norm for punk houses, is a product of limited alternatives for punk bands that wanted to play all-ages shows in Sacramento. "There was a time between 2004 and 2008 where there were literally no all-ages clubs in

Sacramento and it was the only place you could go," claims Mickie. Punks want to play music, hear music, and hang out with friends. Although the term "nightlife" conjures an image of excitement with friends in fun environments, the reality is that in the context of live music, these good times come with multiple personal and collective costs. Even people who are old enough to drink or to get into a bar or club with age limits, understand that the night-life spaces are grounded in an economy that removes money from the scene. Music is often one part of a venue's income, sometimes a larger part and sometimes a very small part. Alcohol sales and perhaps some food sales are often more of a priority for venues because these products are the main income generators. Music becomes a soundtrack for a night out. Cam Myers, who lived in and helped book FSU Garage House, now lives in Minneapolis and says that this use of music as part of a nightlife experience is a recurring problem in his city. Comparing the bar scene to the FSU Garage House, Cam is shocked that "a lot of bar shows here are free, which is kind of strange. I guess they do these shows to get people in to drink." Lack of cover charge, which is usually the source of pay for bands, means those bands won't be paid or are paid based on a percentage of drinks sold. The latter is rare, but when this approach is used, the bands basically become drink sales hustlers instead of focusing on social interactions with people in the bar.

While some bars and clubs are central to alternative and indie rock scenes, booking indie rock bands is not the same as fostering a DIY scene. There are, of course, sonic links between so-called indie or alternative rock bands and DIY punk bands, but I think it's important to avoid conflating sounds with a scene since there are times when the two don't naturally coalesce. Some bands move between bars or clubs and DIY spaces (e.g., White Lung's first shows in Chicago were at houses and Iceage played at a house on their first trip through Chicago but subsequent shows by both bands have been at bars). On the whole, however, a commitment to DIY is reflected in the choices made by people to book DIY spaces, bands to play those shows, and locals to support the bands by regularly attending shows in the spaces. Such efforts become even more important now that an alternative style is no longer distinct from mainstream fashions: thrift store aesthetics feature in a variety of hip chain clothing stores and tattoos and piercings won't distinguish a punk from someone who is more mainstream. If mainstream people look like punks, it's hard to tell which individuals are truly connected to the scene. The house, then, serves another function: it is a material space that can distinguish a DIY punk scene from other alternative music scenes. The space reflects the ideologies that are key to being a punk and believing in DIY. Punks who identify with a DIY philosophy usually know that the house exists (or houses exist), whereas the mainstream person who wants to look the part of a punk will stick to the so-called legitimate venues.

People who live in smaller towns and cities might lack any choices for alternative music, with nightclubs instead booking DJs that spin pop songs or bands that play classic rock covers. "Going back to the beginning, for me the reason for having shows is that we wanted something to do in town for everybody who was interested. There were probably closer to ten bands in high school, which at that point is a lot of bands in the Palmer area," John observes. "It's a lot of kids who don't have cars and can't drive 45 minutes to North Hampton, a place with actual venues, or Springfield." He adds that some official venues were, in the best-case scenario, not tuned in or exploitive. He adds that bands were required to submit demo tapes to some official venues, which was beyond the budgets of kids in that scene. "Or you get roped into some bogus deal where you have to sell 150 tickets. And that's not what it's about at all, so we decided to do it ourselves. So it was a place for our friends to play. And personally I went from playing in six or seven bands to playing in no bands and just bookin' shows. So it wasn't always about me having a place to play, but about friends and bands in town."

One struggle for many punks who do house shows is finding a balance between having a place where local friends and touring bands can play, introducing new people to the music, and not having shows balloon so much that the sense of connection between people in the space is drained to the point that the house becomes as impersonal as the club. When the right balance is fostered, the DIY space can become self-sustaining. "It got to the point where I didn't need to make flyers. I made a little logo and would post the date on-line. But most of the time it would go by word-of-mouth," says Mickie about Casa. "The bands that I booked would tell all their friends and they would tell all their friends. It was exactly the way I wanted it because only the people that gave a shit would be coming to the show, not people who wanted to come and start trouble and get drunk and fuck things up."

Mickie notes that Casa de Chaos is approaching its ten-year anniversary, "which is weird." His surprise stems from the general length of time that that most house spaces last. Punks tend to do things in the moment rather than worrying about the future. If we compare houses to other material features of punk, we can see a consistent focus on the now. For example, people rarely number the first issue of their zines because they are simply thinking about that zine in that moment, not issue number two. Similarly, bands that release their own records aren't identifying as label owners; they're just trying to find a way to get their music heard. When other bands inquire about the label, the band (as label owners) might be shocked. But another reason for Mickie's surprise brings us back to the idea that punk now has a rich history, yet that history is shaped by a collection of ephemeral parts. There are probably as many fanzines as there are magazines and there are so many punk records released each year that it's impossible to keep up with new bands, reissues, and new releases from old bands that have been newly discovered. Albums, 7" singles, 10" records, digital downloads, cassettes, CDs, DVDs, and VHS tapes continue to flood the punk-rock

marketplace. Taken together, punk has a rich living history that is both static and dynamic. But nobody expects it to last at a micro level. The zine will run for a couple issues. The band will break up within two years. The house space will close after a year or two. And then new zines will be published. New bands will form. And new houses will emerge. Individual contributions die off, but punk continues on, sometimes shifting and changing and sometimes new voices seem to be repeating what was said twenty years ago.

Lost Cross is another punk house that seems to defy the temporal norms for house spaces, both because of its longevity and because shows were treated as shows, not as parties (even if the shows at Lost Cross have always had a more chaotic party feel). Patrick Houdek moved to the Carbondale, Illinois area in 1985 when he was fifteen years old. Around that time punks had just started renting the house that would become Lost Cross. "I missed their first show by a week. From then on it was local bands that would play," Patrick tells me about the early days of the house. "Then I started booking bands because I tried to get bands from my tapes." Patrick had been putting out cassette compilations through his P&S Productions label and corresponding with punks throughout the U.S. "I was fifteen, sixteen and getting mail every day. So then I was in touch with bands. We started booking bands with people that we knew, mostly Chicago bands. It got to the point, though, that people started calling that we hadn't heard of. And then in fall of 1987 one of our friends moved into a house in Carbondale, and for a while this was the place that had more shows; it was called House of Voodoo." Having two house spaces seemed to energize the scene, creating more of an underground presence for local punks. "And that's where Carbondale's basement show scene got a lot bigger, because we had a lot of bands. We started getting bands from California, touring bands, whereas before it was more people that somebody knew in Chicago." Eventually Voodoo closed and Lost Cross became the regular house space for DIY shows, continuing to this day.

Lost Cross was not only a place for shows, but also has a history of serving as a spot for punk bands to practice. The transition from a practice space to a show space happens in part because band members are often interested in contributing to DIY scenes in ways that can extend beyond making music.

Al Pist tells me that The Pist did three DIY tours shortly after the band formed. They would return home to Connecticut to their separate apartments and have to pay for a rehearsal space that they shared with some other bands. They sought an economic alternative that would make more sense. They rented a house with a basement so they "had [their] own place to rehearse." Al tells me, "I don't even think there was a conversation that we were going to do shows; it was just sort of a given. We have the spot, let's do a show."

It took a little time to soundproof the basement where they rehearsed and then decided to have a New Year's Eve party. "This was the beginning of '96. For the first show I don't think we put out a flyer necessarily, but we did have a mailing list." Al said the place was called The Pist House and the first show was Aus Rotten, Dropdead, The Pist, and he thinks there might have been a couple local bands as well. "The word got around pretty quick," Al remembers. "It was a word-of-mouth scene." He notes that the shows were always interesting because of the dynamics in the scene. "There weren't a lot of divisions. Punk kids knew each other. There was a schism between the hardcore—jock hardcore scene—and the punk scene, but within the punk scene there were crusties and skinheads. So the shows were pretty well attended most of the time."

The Repos, 09/06, Rancho Huevos, Chicago, IL

The early-to-mid 1990s was a time when houses began to steadily dot the DIY punk show landscape throughout the U.S. Although many of these houses started because punks needed a place for their bands to practice and play, there were some houses that got going because punks wanted to make something happen in their scenes. Club Blitz was a house in Westmont, a southwest suburb of Chicago. It was a go-to destination for "straight edge kids who lived in Westmont and Downers Grove and Elmhurst and who knows where," Kim Nolan remembers. "They were hardcore kids, straight edge kids. Like '88 hardcore. New York style." The space might sound familiar to punks who were (or are) into that style of hardcore because Tony Brummel was one of the residents. In fact, his first Victory Records office was started out of a closet in that house.

Calbee Mundy (known as Chuck Booth at that time) was close with a lot of the people living there. He tells me that the house started "when a lot of the kids graduated from high school and wanted to go out on their own, so they rented this house together." He describes the house as a typical 1970s suburban home, which seemed to be juxtaposed with the aggressive sounds of the bands that played there. Kim Nolan adds that

Club Blitz was definitely a different scene when compared to the basement shows she attended a few years earlier. "Later on when I would go to the Club Blitz shows, those were not parties. I was at Club Blitz because bands were going to play."

This shift away from the party to something more serious was reflected in the quantity and types of shows that happened at Club Blitz. Both Kim and Calbee remember the house being very active with shows, with at least one per week and sometimes two or three. "It was almost always touring bands," Kim remarks. "Either West Coast to East Coast and back or East Coast to West Coast and back. If you're a really small touring band and you're not gonna open for whoever is going to play at the Vic [a 1,400 person capacity venue in Chicago that has some general admission floor space and some seating in the balcony], where do you play? And so one of the things that Club Blitz did was fill the hole for smaller shows for people who were on DIY tours."

Given the style of hardcore that was booked, the punks who were there for shows skewed young. Calbee estimates that the age range was sixteen to twenty-two, adding that there weren't any older punks hanging out. Shows tended to start early and were usually over by 10:00 p.m. But the house didn't last long.

Potty Mouth, 04/22/12, The Whitney House, Hartford CT

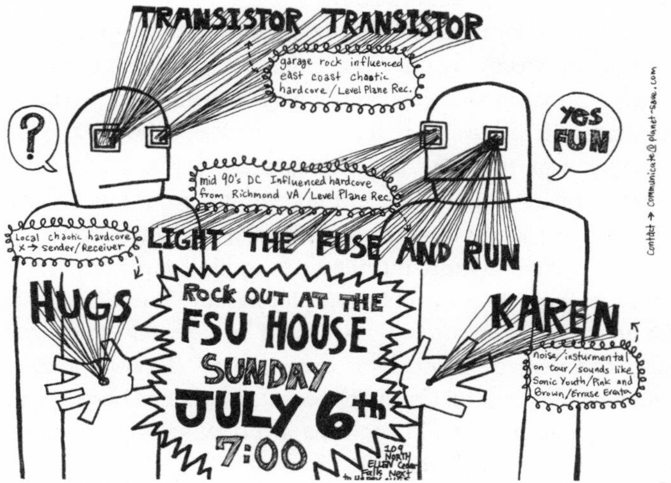

Kim says that by the time she started her freshmen year at college in 1991, the house was done. "Places like that happen for a very short time," Calbee observes. "Basically it happens when kids get out of high school, they get their first place and there are freedoms. It's kind of anything goes. They have shows, and they do stuff, and there's that whole activity of youth, which I experienced a lot in skateboarding and in punk rock."

A teenager might fantasize about being Robert Plant or Janis Joplin but he or she lives a life that is radically different from those rock stars, whereas the punk bands tear down their gear and stand next to the people who were just watching the band play. But this history doesn't explain another crucial feature of the house show: the energy and feel of the house space compared with other show spaces (DIY and mainstream).

Dreams from the Basement

S.H.I.T.'s excellent blend of UK82, D-beat, and raw punk fills the Mousetrap. This Toronto band's demo tape is one of the more exciting releases this year and it's great to hear how that tape translates live. Ryan's reverb-drenched vocals on the demo aren't as wet tonight, but they're still very cool. Meanwhile the guitars are much more fuzzed out and sound more intense compared with the tape. The punks closest to the band slam a little bit, but seem more interested in mixing some pogoing with the moshing. They haven't completely surrounded the singer but he is squeezed into a tight wall of bodies. The show started fairly early for a "bring your own booze" (BYOB) house, but Mousetrap is located in a neighborhood that has been changing fairly rapidly. Houses in the area are now selling for over one million dollars, and the old apartment buildings have been gutted and rehabbed as condos with new brick-façades and large front windows (an aesthetic that seems to be appealing to Chicago's yuppies, who like to put themselves on display). Many of these condos are listed at $500,000. Needless to say, a late-night Sunday show is likely to piss off these neighbors.

Mousetrap has an apartment living space above an old storefront. The bands play on the ground floor, which I assume once housed a bodega or a tavern given the narrow features and black-and-white checkerboard flooring. The sound here is always really good and the somewhat large (by house show standards) rectangular main room combined with a backyard for between-set cool downs in the summer make this one of the city's better places to see a show. Mousetrap has been one of the most consistent show spaces in recent years, hosting three to four shows a month and sometimes more during heavier touring times. It is also one of the more stable spaces in Chicago (perhaps the third longest-running, and among the most consistent since one of those other houses—Rancho Huevos—had not hosted any shows for nearly two years).

Although DIY places have appeared from time to time that, like Mousetrap, offer a different type of spatial experience, most houses in Chicago feature similar designs. Almost all of the houses have stone, brick, or concrete walls and a cement floor. I have only been to one space in recent years that had a partial dirt floor. These basement construction materials should make for a horrible sounding environment, but that is rarely the case. As Cam Myers expresses to me during a discussion about the differences between house shows and other types of spaces: "When you're in a basement, you can feel the guitar in your chest, in your head. That's way better [than a bar], but because you can't hear the vocals, the front person is just kind of a puppet." Cam's reference to buried vocals relates to the quality of the PA at many spaces. Most houses where Cam has attended shows have lacked a quality PA system and since punk bands like to play loud, the vocals are lost in a sea of noise. Luckily many of the houses in Chicago have good PA systems and, if vocals are too low in the mix, the problem is usually a product of the band's making poor choices (mostly guitarists' thinking the guitars should be twice as loud as everything else). Of course, there are unfortunate times when the PA is very poor, not working, or non-existent. I remember seeing The New Yorker (a local screamo band that has since broken up) in the living room of a house called The Moving Castle and feeling so bad for Niko who I am sure would have sounded really cool but we were only listening to an instrumental set. Many of the people I have interviewed who have played shows in Chicago have praised the promoters and spaces here; the scene is mostly well run.

Basement shows tend to be the norm in many Midwestern and Eastern cities because these spaces drown out the sound

Native @ Simple Days, Bloomington, IL 2009

better than other parts of a house. Additionally, one can add soundproofing without worrying about aesthetics or making permanent changes to the space that could lead to losing a security deposit on a rental (i.e., attaching insulation or a second level of drywall to one's living room is going to look horrible and potentially damages the walls). Controlling the sounds in this way can limit noise complaints from neighbors. Also, hosting shows in the basement can provide some separation between a more pseudo-public show space and a private living space in the house or apartment. Of course, basements are not built

Native @ Simple Days, Bloomington, IL 2009

into houses in many U.S. cities or are so small (height and/or square footage) that a show would be impossible. Thus, there are many different types of house spaces that are used by punks in addition to basements. In my experience there's certainly a different sound in basement spaces compared to living rooms or lofts, which tend to have higher ceilings, hardwood floors, and/or are less confined. This combination of bodies spread throughout the space inside the house or loft and the physical design allows the sound to float and might produce a bit more echo in the room compared to a basement.

One thing that cuts across the various house show spaces is a desire to work with what one has at one's disposal, again understanding that these spaces provide the highest level of control for the show promoter. At the same time, each house has its own unique feel, which develops because of the people who live there and the punks who show up. Both groups have ideas about what should happen in their local scenes, and the houses end up reflecting those desires. Moreover, living in the houses with a group of punks and opening one's house to more punks can energize or wear down residents. The overall vibe of each space and experiences in those spaces are also directly linked to choices about running a sober space or hosting BYOB shows.

Economics alone did not lead to the surge in house show options throughout the United States. Instead, the financial benefits rest alongside the experiential features of seeing bands in a house. The raw sounds combine with the feel of a tight space filled with bodies to create a unique atmosphere. Of course, different houses offer different experiences, but there are some qualitative features that cut across many houses.

The bands usually play on the floor, which affects how people interact with band members and one another. Moreover, people in attendance seem a bit more laidback; they don't perform the same kind of public persona that one finds in a club or bar (the back and forth to the bar and the angling to get the bartender's attention, the seeing and being seen, the pickup scene). That's not to say that house shows offer a pure utopian alternative where everyone is tuned into the music at all times or that cliques don't form; rather, the general uses of a house as a place where one can unwind and feel at home seems to transfer to how people act when they attend a house show. If one considers the ways that social interactions happen in many people's living rooms, a similar mood and energy is reflected at a house show. I find it particularly interesting when the living room vibe is transferred to the basement. The basement is a part of the house that most residents usually avoid when possible other than to dump storage items that they think are important (but not important enough to keep in the house) or to access gardening equipment in the summer and snow removal gear in the winter.

Ana Armengod is an artist who has traveled to share her work, and she has toured with friends' bands. These experiences plus her time as a resident at Legion of Doom in Columbus, Ohio inform her assessment of different types of punk spaces. Legion of Doom is one of the longest running houses in the country and is a well-known space among touring punk bands. It is also a house that exists in a scene that has a solid tradition of supporting punk house spaces. "I definitely think it's a bit different. I wouldn't call it better, or anything like that. It's just different," Ana tells me.

Saira Huff, like Ana, believes that "The house show is definitely more like you are just hanging out." She has been in a few different bands, most notably the singer in crust/anarcho-punk band Detestation and most recently the bass player in dark punk band Rosenkopf. "You are totally connected to the 'audience' because you're all together. There's no green room. There's no backstage. You show up and you're right in the midst of things, so I feel like it's a lot more of a communal feeling when you're playing a house because you're all just hanging out," she explains to me.

And Chris Moore notes from the standpoint of playing in hardcore bands that there is an energy at house shows that is not usually replicated in other types of spaces. "Sometimes that feeling that anything could go wrong is something that I would prefer over knowing that 'Oh yeah, this show will be... These bands are gonna play; it's gonna be cool.' It might a little tame, you know. There's enough space for everybody." He adds that this chaos at the house show is tied to not being concerned about capacity, having 125 people, for example, in a space that really has a capacity that is much, much lower.

This general vibe that Ana, Saira, and Chris describe about the house show is a product of active and ongoing efforts among punks to make a scene where people can connect. A house space is not like a bar or club, which are ready-made establishments that were created to earn profit and sometimes to prescribe behaviors. Emily from the band Varix discusses the Rathole house in South Minneapolis during an April 2014 interview with *MRR*. She describes how working to create a space links to a larger commitment to DIY. "They seldom have shows anymore... but I was a part of its beginning," says Emily. "A group of punks spent the entire summer of 2008 getting this condemned and totally fucked up house up to code. Everyone contributed what they could. It was wonderful to experience the motivation and wisdom of punks to achieve a radical living space." Very few houses feature the kind of rehab work that connected Emily to the Rathole, since most house shows happen in rentals that will be mostly liveable.

When Emily and her crew were rehabbing the Rathole in 2008, many other punks throughout the U.S. were moving into houses for the purpose of doing shows. They were contributing to an evolving history of DIY show production and adding more nodes to a touring network. Each new house is a reaffirmation

Summer 1993, Cabbage Collective Show, Calvary Church, West Philadelphia

that alternative approaches to music production, consumption, and economies can work. Similarly, people don't have to rely on mainstream media outlets to learn about bands and their tours. Instead, anyone can create and share through word-of-mouth, on-line forums and in the past via resources like *Book Your Own Fuckin' Life*.

Taken together, the communal feel and relaxed vibe of a house space reflect one aspect of the house show experience, but these features blend with an intense energy that results from the compact nature of the spaces. "We tended to do shows from March or April to November, but we did do two or three shows in the winter and I'm talking, like I was outside collecting money and I was standing on a chair. I couldn't sit in the chair because there was that much snow," John Boilard tells me about the Shed. "We shoveled a pathway. We only had two or three bands play and it was probably one of the best shows we've ever done there. I think between 60 and 100 people showed up and it was so hot in the shed that people were almost naked by the time the second band played. It was very strange. If someone had opened the door and had no idea that these shows were happening, they probably would freak out: 'What is going on in here? Everyone is sweaty, half-naked, and a band is playing.'"

John describes an experience that reminds us about the different types of punk shows that happen at houses. There can

Big Eyes, 06/04/13, 86 Mets, Chicago, IL

be a romantic feeling that features in some spaces, especially when emo bands or pop punk bands are playing. More people can dance because there isn't a pit and more people sing along (rather than screaming along). The music is less aggressive, which means fewer men have claimed the front space.

The hardcore show offers its own unique experience, as Dave Zukauskas describes in reference to the music's dynamic energy. He explains this spirit in the context of photographing bands. "One of the nice things about basement shows is that everything is packed in so tight. When you've got the crowd pushed up against the band, it adds an extra element. And the singer is often standing in the first couple rows of people." The energy of the show is made more intense because the bands play on the floor, which means "you're eye-to-eye with the band," observes Dave. "You also get the crowd's facial expression. You'll get someone who is singing along and so their mouth is open and eyes are squinting. They got a fist in the air, an emotion is being expressed that adds something to the background of the photo."

Dave's photographs, and those of other punks who share their work through zines, blogs, and the occasional book, provide a visual counterpart to the music. Photography has been central to punk's cultural history. The photos show us what's happening, providing visible evidence of the ways that scenes have changed and/or stayed the same over time. The images from punks like Dave record the chaos and dynamism of punk shows and can entice others who seek an experience that can accompany the sounds.

The combination of laid-back feel and chaotic energy is often experienced in different ways in the sporadic collection of spaces that have emerged throughout the country. Some of the people in the past had a clear plan when it came to booking shows, while others were figuring it out as they went along. The rationale for these choices helped influence the feel of the space and contributed to the dynamics of the local scenes. In some instances punks created DIY spaces because they wanted to foster a more engaged and safe scene; they needed an alternative to what had been accepted as common practice in their scenes. For example, Saira's personal punk history in Portland is tied to a social history of punk that was deeply linked to a new vision of DIY that emerged in the early 1990s and informs much of what happens with DIY spaces today. "I was disgusted by the older punks in Portland. Poison Idea were the older punks, and I was just like, 'Oooh. I don't want anything to do with anybody like that.' And also they were playing huge shows, where I would always get beat up by a skinhead," she remembers. "So the Portland DIY scene in the late '80s/early '90s was sort of a reaction to the older punks. Like, 'You guys have no accountability or ethics.' They didn't care if Nazis came to the show, if you got beat up, if the show was expensive. They just didn't care." It is likely that some of the punks who were not happy with that scene did what some punks always do: they complained. Others worked to create an alternative. "In Portland they were kind of like, 'Fine, we're just gonna do something else.' And they did, and that's the scene that I came up into." These efforts by Saira and other punks in the Portland scene were not isolated. Punks throughout the U.S. were working toward the production of spaces that could reflect and foster punk communities grounded in links between DIY and a more egalitarian cultural politics.

Although punk is often discussed inside and outside the scene as a music and culture that is intertwined with DIY, there are various approaches to punk and not all are committed to DIY in the same ways. The sound of a crunchier hardcore band from one city, for example, might be similar to a hardcore band from another city. But the similarities end with the sounds when the two bands chase radically different goals and attract different crowds. The scenes are different even if the sounds are similar. Not all punk bands are committed to a DIY scene.

Tim Yohannan argued in his June 1994 *MRR* column that three criteria distinguish truly independent punk from the rest of the bands lumped into punk categories: "1) It doesn't really matter what you say or what you sing, but how you conduct your business and what your motivation for doing it is. 2) It is only by being completely separated from government control and corporate sponsorship, collusion, or connections that one can really claim to be 'alternative' or 'independent.' 3) Unless there is an ongoing class consciousness to one's communication and expression, then it is inventible that you will be assimilated into mainstream values, no matter how culturally 'hip' you attempt to be." Tim Yo's assessment of independence in that column was a response to the rise of major label interest in punk bands and the swallowing up of independent distribution outlets by those same corporations. It was very difficult at that time for bands to navigate the production and distribution climate if they wanted to get their records into stores and avoid corporations, but his ideas can also be applied to the context of shows and touring then and now.

Making a DIY scene, which is in part linked to the emergence of a house show network, reflects a shift in what it meant to do and be punk, especially after the first cycle of punk music and culture started to stabilize in the U.S. (i.e., some bands could play larger venues and sell enough records to earn a living, festivals were starting to take shape that could draw huge crowds, and commercial radio stations were adding bands to playlists). Punks began to reconsider their goals and how they could work within a DIY ethos. Chris Terry, who sang in Light the Fuse and Run and created the *Gullible* fanzine, tells me about the aspirations of his first band that played out regularly: Flesh Eating Creeps. "We wanted to play the house shows. They seemed like the coolest," Chris says. "It probably took us at least a year. By the end of high school we'd gotten to know more people, 'cause the house shows were more based around college. High school kids were

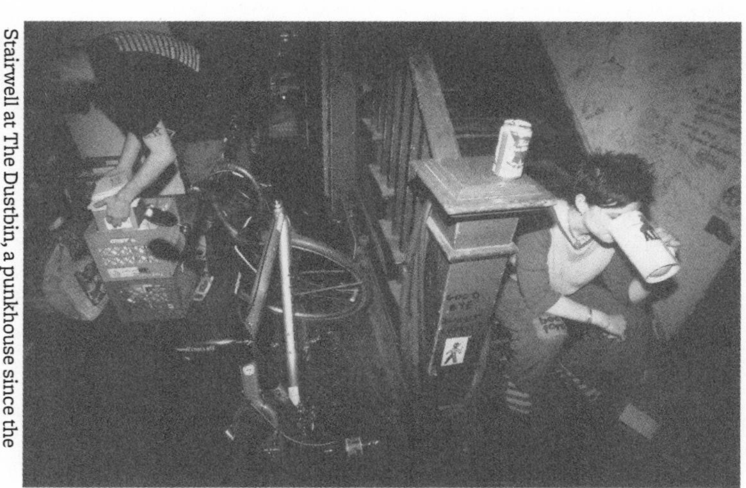

Stairwell at The Dustbin, a punkhouse since the 1970s in Portland, OR, May 2000

more likely to go to all-ages shows at clubs or there was a church called Saint Edwards that had a rec area where bands played. So there was that kind of separation by age but as we got closer to college, we were more tapped into that. We knew more friends who had their own places to live where we could play."

Aiming to play houses is certainly a sign that a band is committed to DIY punk, but this approach to sharing music is radically out of step with mainstream ideas about live music. Many people I've interviewed for this book or whom I know in bands have shared stories with me about conversations with family members, co-workers, and/or non-punk friends at school. Those people are constantly surprised by the goals of a DIY tour: to play music, to travel, and meet new people. "Wait, you mean to tell me that you are going on tour for five days and will play in people's basements in Indiana, Michigan, Ohio, and then come back?! You won't make any money?" go the stories told to me. They want to know about fame and fortune, groupies and drugs, and light shows. They think the punks are naïve because a DIY approach to music isn't connected to some kind of end goal (i.e., "making it"). Bull Gervasi suggests that there is in fact something bigger happening during a DIY tour, but still those experiences would not fit with expectations of progress. Policy of 3 went on their first national tour in the summer of 1993. "I remember we played 21 shows in 38 days, which was far less than what we intended to play," Bull explains to me. They had hoped to play every day. "We knew we wouldn't be making any money, so we were trying to play as much as we could." Despite the usual van problems and some last-minute cancellations, he considers that experience to be transformative. "It was a great tour, too, in that it made me fall in love with traveling and seeing new places, meeting new people. I graduated from high school in '92. I didn't go to college but I feel like I learned so much from being self-sufficient and having to deal with these new situations: getting along with four people you are stuck in a van with, coming up with creative solutions to breaking down in weird places, having to deal with having barely any money on the road and being 3,000 miles from home. It was an absolute life changing experience, and we met so many great people that I am still friends with to this day."

Zines for sales at Mauled by Tigers Festival in Chicago, August 2008

But if Bull was able to view touring as an end goal in itself, others have not been so expansive in their thinking. Joe Milik books shows at his house in Iowa City and is the drummer in Nerv (among other bands). He underscores how mainstream attitudes about so-called correct ways to do live music also influence some people who identify as punks. Joe tells me about the first house space where he lived, which was an old office building in Des Moines, Iowa that he and his roommates named the Haunted Basement (even though bands did not play the basement). When they started hosting shows, the small room where bands would play was regularly packed. Then attendances started to dip. "I feel people had certain stigmas about the place because it was not a music venue. I think that kept a lot of people away that would have been interested in some of the bands that we booked," Joe asserts. "If we would have booked them at a legitimate, actual, lawful venue, more people would have been interested in it. The deal with that, though, is that we thought we could get more money to the bands if we could book it, because we don't have to pay the bar or the soundman or the doorman."

Although some punks internalize normative ideas about where live music should happen, others develop a deeper commitment to punk because of the ideals that are enacted in DIY punk show spaces. Jake from the bands Parasol MA and Peeple

Watchin' explains to me, "For me, growing up in a shitty suburb I was just feeling so alienated from everything and feeling so shitty about everything. But just having this feeling, and who knows where it comes from, but having this adventurous personality where I am looking for something else, not just in the sense that here's a bunch of bands that are playing in a basement but they were a bunch of bands that wanted to play in basements."

Jake, like so many other punks, narrates the basement as a crucial feature of DIY as a cultural politic. Sometimes the political ideologies are linked to a far more explicit and familiar type of action (e.g., a benefit show that raises money for a local fest, a table that has anarchist literature, a show that follows a skillshare or really really free market). But more often, punk politics are enacted in everyday life. Adam from Porcelain Decay notes in *Between Resistance and Community* that the Long Island DIY scene "doesn't necessarily have the tools for unionizing workers or anything like that, but it has the tools for creating community and for educating." Some punks are drawn to the music and culture because of the politics, most find the music first and the cultural politics later, and others grow into some combination of art and politics.

Clay Dehann tells me that his first tour experience helped shape his sense of what was possible with house shows. His band Red Versus Black toured from upstate New York, where he was attending college, to Denver (his home town). "We played houses, we played some record stores, loft type things."

He explains that the tour was rough in terms of money, but the opportunity to play at and learn about DIY spaces was transformative. "So after that tour I moved into a co-op in Ithaca, New York. We had regular shows there. In the back there was a building that was an old slaughterhouse, so we called it the Abattoir." Clay was able to learn about DIY spaces through this tour, while other punks develop an understanding of houses through a rich local scene.

"Basements in particular were a big part of what got me into it, and I guess I didn't realize how much didn't revolve around basements until I got older," Zack Furness tells me. "Older" meant post-college after he left a thriving scene in State College, Pennsylvania. His house hosted pop punk and ska shows. "There was also a house that I think was just called the White Lodge. One of the guys played in a bunch of regionally pretty well known emo bands and had a lot of connections with folks in Jersey and New York. Ted Leo came and played his house right after Chisel broke up." Then there was another house that two women booked that "had all the really crusty political bands play their kitchen, which was really tiny." Given these options, it's easy to see why Zack assumed that his rich house scene was mirrored in other U.S. cities. Many people who have houses in their scenes will think that doing house shows is a no-brainer. And others learn about this DIY show option because there is much more talk about house shows in various punk media now compared to the past, which means more punks will learn about the viability of doing house shows.

"It's hard to recognize the importance and impact a space or idea can have on you until you step away from it. A few days ago, I realized I was standing in a basement that truly changed my life for the last time ever. For the past year and a half, I lived in a humongous punk house located in Columbus, OH named Villa Villekulla," writes Emmy Ramone in an October 2014 *MRR* guest column. The house embodies DIY, providing a location where community can be created and sustained for some and a place to grow into punk for others. Of course, there is a third group made up of people who are merely passing through punk on their way to something else, but ideally these folks develop an understanding that individuals can make and share their own forms of culture rather than relying on the culture industry. "While it just served as a venue for us to do our thing, it really left its mark on the way we did it for the last few years," Emmy adds. "It still will be a great way to look back on a point in my life where we all really did some livin." Emmy's column explicitly and implicitly speaks to the distinctions between a house and a home.

In punk rock circles, the house is transformed when local punks use the space to hang out and see bands. The material features don't change much just because the house becomes a venue, but punks imbue the house with meaning through actions and the communication that surrounds the house. The term "house" is always used in reference to a show space: punk house, house show, house venue. But these phrases connote more than a mere domicile. The term "house" is therefore used in a way that reflects the meaning of "home," which finds a parallel in other languages. For example, my friend Octavio, who is teacher in Portugal, tells me that there is a similar difference between a house ("casa") and a home ("lar") in Portuguese. "However, we tend to use 'lar' quite rarely, because 'casa' usually means the building and also the place where you feel at home," he tells me. "We usually say, 'Aqui, sinto-me em casa' which means 'Here, I feel at home.'" The house is a home in this Portuguese phrase in the same way that the punk house is a home for renters who live there but also for bands that play shows and people in the scene.

The language we use to represent our spatial encounters both reflects and helps shape those experiences. One interesting link between language and experience can be seen in the names that punks adopt for their houses. James Payne writes in a guest column for *MRR* in January 2013 that there are five categories for names that punks should consider if they are going to host house shows. First, there are geographical references, which James claims to be "boring but effective" since the name is either the address and street name or just the street name. Next, an in-joke among people in the house can lead to a name. Although other people rarely understand the joke, "it's usually such a distinctive name that everyone is instantly aware of" the house. The third category James discusses is "The Brand." He notes that this category is somewhat ironic given punk's aversion to

Los Crudos, 03/02/13, ChiTown Futbol, Chicago, IL

marketing, but this class of names is especially important if the space needs to stand out. Branding is particularly useful if the house is going to be used for more than just shows. A zine fest or skillshare, for example, would seek to attract a group of folks who might not normally attend house shows but share punk's ethos. A good Chicago example would be Swerp Mansion, which was a loft space. The show space was linked to a DIY label and also the location for a fest. Fourth, is serendipity. James claims that some punks believe "that any pre-meditated thought process regarding a proper moniker is bad luck, an omen of future trouble whether that takes the form of scabies, negligent roomies, or missing mic cables." Instead, the house takes on a name over time, although James warns that such an approach can lead to a name that might be insulting (e.g., Flooded Toilet House). Finally, there are houses named after the people who live there: "Your Name + House." He warns against this choice because a successful house will likely outlast that person whose name is used. James lists Legion of Doom as an example here. Had the house been named after one of the early residents the moniker would be less fitting once that punk moved out, whereas Legion of Doom still exists and retains a unique name.

My conversations with various people about their current or former houses feature explanations that align with James' categories. For example, Joe Milik explains that "the Haunted Basement actually started out as a place we called the Secret Spot because we were afraid that our landlord was gonna find out about it if we published the address. For the first few months it was pretty much a word-of-mouth thing." Then the name changed but Joe can't remember why they decided on Haunted Basement. "It was kind of called that on a whim, as a joke," he tells me. "I don't know what our thought process was. But there were no shows in the basement. The basement was like a ten by ten room that was pretty much a sewer. Nobody ever went down there." I am guessing that an in-joke about the basement's grimy qualities led to the name given Joe's explanation, whereas the Secret Spot was far more literal.

Patrick Houdek remembers that the first time he met people who were living at Lost Cross was Halloween 1986. "I have a flyer for the week before and it says Lost Cross house on it. What I understand is that there was a band Blood Stained Tools but before that they were called Lost Cross and they had somebody that lived there who helped write and it was about losing a cross earring, so they just used that." Of course, many of the houses are named after the band that started the house as a practice space and then expanded to host shows.

The experiences of residents and local punks in a scene that inform a house moniker are important beyond the name. That is, the name of a house, like the stories that are told about a scene (either informally via word of mouth or shared out to punks in other scenes via various DIY media) emerge from a combination of everyday interactions in the space, which will include a mix of agreed upon amazing shows, average shows, and a collection of mostly forgettable bands. These experiences both develop from and reflect how the house functions as a venue and also links to residents' goals for their houses. The people I interviewed mostly describe positive features of living in a punk house that also serves as a show space, but they are also very much aware of the fact that such ways of living together aren't enjoyable for everyone. Some of the excitement and the problems are directly connected to forms of communal or pseudo-communal living, but other positive and negative features are tied to hosting shows.

"The house went through different names and went through different people, but it has been inhabited by punks and weirdos since the '70s," Ana tells me about Legion of Doom. She notes that the current name and general approach to doing shows began in September 1996. At the time I spoke with Ana there were six people living in the house and three handled most of the booking. "But we try to make everyone responsible for shows even if you aren't booking shows, it's not your show, and

Native, Simple Days, Bloomington, IL, 2009

it might not be of your interest. It's still the house that you live in. Living in a punk house that's also a venue, as much as I don't like calling it that, there's responsibilities. Everyone who moves here knows that and is aware of that part of living here."

James Payne also lives in Columbus. He has helped with the founding of multiple houses that did shows prior to moving to Skylab, a more community-focused art space, where he currently books bands. "When you do it in your house, there is such a charged meaning to it. There's a certain idea of intimacy," he says. "It's a lot about trust, I guess. Galleries are nice but I can't even compare them. You have an event at a gallery or a store and it's about padding someone's CV or moving some books or whatever. There's no amount of things I could ever do in my own punk house that would ever pad my CV." It's important to remember the broad spectrum of music that falls under the punk umbrella when considering this notion that an art gallery show could pad a promoter's vita. Organizing pop punk or hardcore shows in a gallery space probably won't help with grant funding or artist-in-residency appointments, but a noise band could be linked to an avant-garde performance of some kind. Similarly, a festival that blends punk music, experimental sound art, and documentary photography, for example, could be funded through a non-profit agency.

James is referencing the general feel of the show space by mentioning the intimate nature of the house show, but he's also broadening out this idea to reflect on the ways that people in the punk house live together. He observes that the people with whom he lived "looked exactly the same; they all wore the same clothes. It's not something they came into. They'd all been around each other so much that it was kind of like there was this set of opinions that they have, a set of ways that they look at the world. It's really interesting that you are actively able to build that and have it be successful, but it's also one of the things that really alienated me from it because I just always had other interests."

Chris Terry tells me that he lived at the 805 W. Carey house in Richmond, Virginia with seven to eight other people at any given time, which he says was about average when he thinks about the houses where he saw shows or his bands played.

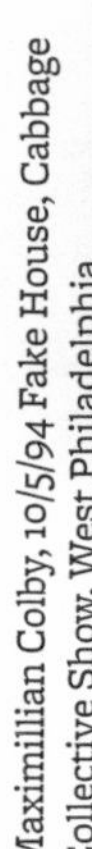
Maximillian Colby, 10/5/94 Fake House, Cabbage Collective Show, West Philadelphia

Younger people have less money and are more interested in the social features that accompany collective living (unlike older people who tend to seek more private domestic spaces shared with family members). Ana notes, for example, "Obviously when people moved into this house, since it was something they started together, it was a different feeling. Like, the house probably meant more for them." She was very attracted to living with other punks in a show space and only decided to move out because she wanted to return to Mexico City. But not everyone can sustain the same excitement about living in a punk house. "The whole time I've lived here we've gone through so many roommates," Ana explains, reflecting on her time at Legion of Doom. She understands that the reasons people leave are diverse, but adds: "Not everyone who lives here has the same sense of wanting to be involved with the house, which can be sort of sad because this space is so important to me."

Usually people choose to live in a punk house because of opportunities to reside with like-minded people, the rent is cheap, and being in the midst of the punk rock action is exciting. For example, Annie Rose tells me that she moved into Casa de Chaos in Sacramento, California when she was nineteen years old. She wanted to live in section of the city that was more interesting (an area known as the Barmuda Triangle, according to Mickie Rat) while looking to avoid the higher rents for apartments in that neighborhood. Because there were six people living in Casa, the rent was not very high. "I had been to the basement shows before and I knew it was a fun place to hang out," says Annie. "The house was in pretty bad shape when I moved in but all the roommates were cool and the place is in a great location."

Most houses will fold once the people living there move out, but Patrick Houdek describes why that has not been the case for Lost Cross, "There have been a lot of other basements in Carbondale, but Lost Cross just stayed. Now when someone is moving out, they find somebody who understands: you're gonna have shows; you're gonna have bands practicing; and if there's a show at a bar, when the bar closes people are gonna want to party afterwards. This is your life if you want to live here. Now they [former Lost Cross residents who are still in Carbondale] really look for that commitment." This plan formed after the house nearly folded due to a combination of renters not wanting to host shows and unpaid rent by some tenants.

There is a broad spectrum of houses that host shows. Some are distinct because of the bands that are booked. Others stand out because of a unique experience (e.g., seeing a band in a shed or in a former office building). And some houses can be distinguished from others because of the ways residents and local punks use the spaces.

Ana describes Legion of Doom as a well-organized and politically engaged house (e.g., although residents do not need to be vegan, residents and guests can only cook vegan food in the house). And Legion of Doom is a sober space. By contrast, Annie notices that the people who end up living at Casa the longest "are usually men who are laid-back enough to not care too much about the condition of the house or the constant noise from band practices." Given these living conditions, she says that it "can be difficult to find new roommates because most people don't want to live in such a trashy place." Although she doesn't fit her own description of the longer-term residents, Annie continues to stick around. "I'm actually not the greatest fit because I care more about cleanliness than any of the other roommates and I have anxiety issues during shows."

How residents use the house space and interact with one another is partially influenced by the design of the house.

Space matters. Construction choices influence social uses, which combine to affect social relationships among residents themselves, residents and punks who attend shows, and residents and the bands that play in the house. The importance of design is an issue that resonates with George Myers when he considers the difference between the Schoolhouse in Hadley, Massachusetts and the house that he has lived in and booked after he left the Schoolhouse. George tells me that he and his roommates started doing shows at the Schoolhouse in 2001, focusing on noise bands and the more avant-garde sounds on the punk spectrum. "We moved out of the Schoolhouse in 2004. A lot of us were really fried. That place has two stories but the second floor had been added in the '70s so the building had floor to ceiling windows. There was no privacy. Everyone knew everyone's sex life, what music they were listening to, every single detail was publicly available. It was pretty exhausting." George distinguishes between the lack of privacy that came with living at the Schoolhouse versus privacy issues in the more traditionally designed house he lives in now. "It's a five-bedroom big house. There's good separation between you and your roommates that you would expect: a wall and a full floor [laughs]. The Schoolhouse lacked those things. There was always the sense that you were not just in a shared space, but other people were in your private space."

On one side of an overly simplified dualism, we find punk to be a very organized, well-run, politically savvy, egalitarian culture with various sub-genres of music that reflect that culture. On the other side, punk is destructive, politically grounded in a vision of fucking all authority, and striving to do the opposite of choices that would be made by mainstream people no matter what. An aversion to dirty houses, filthy basements, and a quest for shared responsibility with some degree of privacy is at odds with a vision of the house as a temporary location in which upkeep should not be a concern. These two different approaches can change over time. As Joe Steinhardt from Don Giovanni Records tells Katy Otto in a January 2015 *MRR* interview, "Originally I was attracted to punk because it gave me this kind of space to be angry, offensive, sometimes violent, and basically a jackass to people." He notes that at that time, such choices appeared to be okay because punks in his New Jersey scene seemed to have an implicit agreement that this is what punks did. "But what kept me in punk after I became a little more mature is what I feel is more important about punk as a movement." Joe identifies punk as a "platform for change and a space for learning from people much smarter than yourself and interacting with them directly." This more communal feature compared to the aggressive social interactions is far more appealing, he claims.

Interestingly, the punks in the first camp—a group who wants well-run and community-focused shows—display a vision of the punk house that is very much in line with common approaches to private residences even if the day-to-day life in those punk houses is radically different from the average mainstream household. "I think it's important for people to know that it's your house. At the end of the day, when you shut the door and everyone leaves, it's your house," claims Ana. "If people are disrespectful with your space, and they steal things or they trash things or just do whatever they want, it ends up being on you and that takes a toll on you. There's only so much you can take with people not respecting your space. You'll wake up one day and be like, 'I just don't want to do this anymore.' That's definitely one of the things to consider. At the end of the day, even though the house is the community's, it's also our house and where we live."

Ana is not alone in her assessment of the blurry line between one's private residence and the role one's house can play as a pseudo-public space. Nicole Pagowsky explains to me that she shifted her attention from booking shows in her house to co-organizing a fest at University of Wisconsin, Madison, where she was a student. She liked that with the fest she could go home when the day was done, but that was not the case with shows in her house. "I was just getting tired of having people in my house all the time; it sounded like a great idea at first," she explains. "I had people using my hair stuff. And my former roommate came over with a bottle of Jameson. He tripped and spilled it all over my records."

That fine line between the public and private dimensions of one's house also extends beyond the living spaces. "We tend to get a crazy amount of people here and I worry about the house

Policy of Three 8/16/93 THD House Minneapolis

getting fucked up, like last weekend when a pipe on our water heater was damaged and we ended up with no hot water for three days," Annie tells me. "People get a little too violent in the pit and it takes its toll on the basement." Mickie Rat adds that this dilemma with the water heater started during the second iteration of shows at Casa and was a major source of concern for people in the house. "That was always a problem because on stage left in front of one of the speaker mains is the house water heater. Over the course of several shows when people wanna start pits, they start bashing into the water heater. The next day when you get up and you have to go to work, there's no hot water. You go downstairs and find that the water heater has been broken by people who were repeatedly smashing into it at the punk show. So we started getting someone who had the job of water heater spotter. They stand in front of the water heater and push the flying punks away from it. That person was usually me. But after a while, I'm like, 'Fuck this' and I built a rudimentary wooden cage around the water heater so that people would slam into the cage and we would still have hot showers in the morning. We'd put all sorts of nasty signs and stuff on it. We always had to remind people: 'Please don't run into the water heater.' We've had singers dropkick it and shit like that."

Shotmaker, 7/8/94 Ft. Worth, TX House Show

Although hosting shows can take a toll on some residents, the general energy that surrounds seeing good bands outweighs the downside of opening up one's house. As George notes, the day-to-day life at the Schoolhouse was actually more difficult than at shows. There was an understanding and expectation that the private space would be opened up when the Schoolhouse hosted shows. Plus, "everyone was just excited because these were shows that didn't have a market appeal that could be justified at clubs or you wanted to make them all ages or things that came together quickly. People were supportive of all the things that came along with doing that."

Where the bands play (basement, inside the house, or the backyard) and where people hang out when bands aren't playing (basement, living room, front porch, backyard) contribute to the experience of house shows for residents. For example, Ana says that the ground floor of Legion of Doom had become more of a public space for a few different reasons. First, until the landlord did some work to create a functioning side door to the basement, bands had to bring their gear through the front door, into the living room, and then down to the basement. Now they can get directly to the basement. But then there are the shows. "When people come to our shows, they hang out in our kitchen and our living room," says Ana. "We don't have a backyard. Our side door goes to the alley. But we try to prevent people from going to the alley to avoid annoying our neighbors." She adds that they don't let people go to the second or third floors, which is where most of the bedrooms are located. "I think that there's certain things that you have to be able to cope with, living in a place like this. There's a constant flow of people coming and going. There's always bands in your living room. And you need to be more outgoing to be able to engage with them. You don't want to make them feel awkward. It's awkward enough being in someone else's house, sleeping on their floor."

Specific choices made by people who live in the house and attend shows there can help shape the experience of the house within a scene. As Zack Furness notes, "For me, that [house shows] was one of the things that made punk fun. More than anything, the politics of doing DIY shows is sort of in the background to the fact that basement shows were always a really good time." Many of the people I interviewed echo this sentiment that the house show can be fun, a connection that was not often used to describe other types of DIY spaces.

Although most people I interviewed were unaware of the history of house shows as parties, that general party experience has been preserved even as more consistent DIY efforts are normalized throughout the U.S. compared to the one-off parties that dominated in the past. That is, punks now talk about house shows, not parties. However, when asked to identify some unique features of the house show compared to shows in other DIY spaces, the term "party" is often used or the experience of a party regularly features in descriptions of house shows.

"I think the main difference is that house shows feel more like a big party. My backyard and basement are small so everybody is in there together, there are usually no cliques of people off the side ignoring everybody else, or getting drunk in a parking lot," Annie tells me. "I have more fun at shows at my house than anywhere else because I always meet new people and there doesn't seem to be any barrier between the bands and the audience. Also, everybody can afford to get drunk instead of paying expensive bar prices!"

Clay Dehann explains to me that after the relative success (in punk terms) of the Abattoir, his return to Denver was guided by "the vague idea that we were going to start a house venue somewhere." That plan came to fruition when he and his friends started renting what they named Mouth House. Clay says that there were twelve people living in the house. Cheap housing was ideal for the combination of college students and recent college grads living there. He describes the experience of Mouth House as falling "somewhere between a college party house and a musician co-op. We have aspects of both. A lot of times people will come over to drink and party, but then we also have the more community aspect to it, which is what I am into: having a space for touring bands and a place for local bands that can't play clubs (maybe they're too young and need all ages shows)."

The Dallas/Fort Worth/Denton scene is described by Al Rios as somewhat similar to the blended atmosphere of Mouth House. "If you're having a house show, it's a party. You're gonna get drunk and there's gonna be the expectation that a house show is BYOB." Volunteer-run 1919 Hemphill is the only sober DIY space in that scene right now, claims Al. "House shows are always party shows. I personally don't drink, but it would be super weird to go to a house show and have nobody drinking."

Most people who live in BYOB houses allow drinking because the shows feel a bit looser. In theory, less money spent on drinks means folks have more money to support the bands (buying merch, not getting bent out of shape if there are multiple touring bands on the bill and the suggested donation is higher than the somehow frozen in time $5).

"I love house shows but at the same time that party atmosphere kind of bums me out sometimes," Lily from Parasol MA tells me. "I think that a lot of times it seems like people who have house shows are really stressed out about it, about it being in their home. I mean, I would be, too. As an aware person of my space, I always think that sucks for that person." Although this stress that Lily describes is applicable to any house show, since sober spaces can also be wrecked during shows, stuff can be stolen, and neighbors can complain, BYOB shows tend to be more chaotic. "It's also a hard time living in a house that you're having shows at because you're like, this rules but there's 50 or 60 kids in your house drinking, being disrespectful. Not always, but it happens," Jenny Ray says to me. Her bedroom was upstairs so she had an opportunity to distance herself from the less-private shared living space where the bands played, but she remembers a few times when she would walk downstairs the next day with "this cold, desolate feeling of 'Oh god' because of the wasteland of beer bottles and cans and dirt. But it was always so worth it, like 'Man, that show last night was awesome.'"

Jenny was able to look past the chaos that could ensue at the Bike House, but other punks have felt that there can be ways that shows cross the line from a fun party to a potential source of concern. "The reason we stopped doing shows there was because it got to the point where there were a lot of younger kids coming and kind of using that as a spot to get fucked up," Al Pist tells me about the Panic House. "There were a lot of teen centers around that did shows and they obviously couldn't do that there. So this was like going to a house where they could party without getting yelled at." Al says that he found this scenario to be disturbing and the overall experience was running counter to his goals for the house: hosting touring and local bands and helping make a scene in Connecticut. "After a few shows with that kind of thing happening, we decided to make it no alcohol at the house. And people stopped coming." Al notes that they continued booking the same types of bands and because nobody in the house drank, this shift to a sober space was less hassle for them. But "it made us see, 'Wow, alcohol is really important in this scene. People will not come to shows if they can't drink.' It was kind of a rude awakening."

And here is the rub: Clay's description of Mouth House as one part college party and one part music community is a mix that might be more extreme than most BYOB punk houses. At some point, though, people in each BYOB house will have to make a choice about which type of experience is going to be prioritized: the show or the party. Such choices are connected to the kind of scene punks want to foster in their areas. If people stopped coming to shows at the Panic House because the house became a sober space then one would need to question the commitment of people in that scene to their scene and to DIY punk more generally. This response by the punks in Connecticut demonstrates that perhaps the old model of a punk party (a party with a punk rock soundtrack) is what people in Al Pist's scene wanted.

Saira shares some of the same concerns raised by Al, speaking more explicitly to the problems with playing BYOB shows. "I liked it when places wouldn't allow drinking. For me the fact that people were way more serious about going to a show. It wasn't as big of a deal that they couldn't drink. They weren't just going to party." But she considers this attitude to be the true alternative rather than the norm that is BYOB. "I don't think most people even care that there's a show going on. I would hear people bitch, 'Ohhhh, you can't drink there,'" she says adopting a whiny grumbling tone to mimic the complainers. "You can't wait twenty minutes for a punk set to be over to go have a beer. It kind of separated for me who actually cared about the creativity and who just cared about the party."

Nevin Marshall adds an interesting twist to this argument that reminds me of an article written by Eileen Luhr for *American Studies*. In "Metal Missionaries to the Nation," Luhr notes that 1980s Christian heavy metal bands described sex, drugs, and rock and roll as a norm in rock music culture. These Christian metal bands claimed that they offered a true alternative, a more honest vision of rebellion. Nevin describes something similar.

"Those crazy house shows are much more a replication of capitalism. Everyone has corporate beer (PBR and Bud Light). Everyone's smoking corporate cigarettes. At those houses there's certainly no anti-capitalist analysis going on. It's like, 'We got cheap beers, let's slam these, rage, and mosh,'" says Nevin imitating a sort of jock mentality. "If they showed up with craft brews and were rolling their own cigarettes then maybe. They're not supporting some of the worst companies in the world; that's good. But it's almost universally corporate beer, corporate cigarettes." The metal missionaries argued for a connection with Jesus through metal as an alternative to the mainstream rock culture lifestyle. But Nevin is more concerned with the links between DIY punk and community; those communal connections are undone when punks are more worried about getting fucked up.

He adds that there is another level of social responsibility linked to the distinctions between sober spaces and BYOB houses, which is the possible presence of teenagers. Punks do house shows in part because these types of shows are alternatives to age-restricted bars and clubs. Kids can find out about punk in more ways now than at any point in the past. Most DIY bands have an on-line presence and even many fanzines complement print runs with supplemental content on the web. But finding punk bands and seeing punk bands is not the same thing, since cities with a lot of age-restricted clubs in effect limit all-ages shows to large venues, which are much less intimate than DIY shows. While older punks seem to be generally excited about younger punks learning about DIY cultural politics through the punk show, there has to be an understanding that the BYOB show might not be ideal for such punk rock pedagogy.

Macklin Brundage booked shows in McHenry County (a county made up of rural and suburban towns located about halfway between Chicago and Milwaukee) before moving to Chicago. His shows were primarily attended by kids in high school. "A lot of people see that as a negative thing, something to be laughed at," Macklin says about suburban punk shows. "But I think it's a totally intimidating environment for a fourteen-year-old to go to a show where there are twenty year olds and 30-year-old adults drinking beer and stuff." I asked him if he thinks that intimidation diminishes when shows are held at sober spaces. "When I first started going to Chicago shows they were at places like Summer Camp, which was a sober space. Those spaces have a different appeal. Shows that have drinking and stuff, you can hang out; it's better to go to the show to hang out and not necessarily to go to a show. So I think that's [sober space] a more welcoming environment."

Another interesting issue to consider is a transformation that happens for punks as they age. Matt "Vic" Vicars was in his mid-teens when he started going to shows at the Fort House in Omaha, Nebraska. The experience was transformative because he was able to see many of his favorite bands (e.g. Funeral Diner, Ampere). Like many young punks, he couldn't believe that bands that had released records were playing a "shitty little basement." Vic realized that he and his friends could put on shows as well, which happened fairly quickly. A girl he knew told him that he could do a show in her basement if he and his friends helped her clean the junk out of the space (subcontracting a chore that her parents required). He can't remember if her parents were home when the show happened, but he assumes that they were there. He adds that the parents wouldn't have had much to worry about given their priorities at that time. "When I lived in my own house [Ghost House] and did shows for years and years, there was that party element," Vic tells me. There were often people at shows who weren't part of the scene; they came to his house because they thought a party was going on and just assumed that the band was providing a soundtrack. "This might just be nostalgia or maybe naiveté, but there was none of that," Vic says, thinking back to that first show he booked in his friend's basement. "We were sixteen and didn't care about drinking. We just wanted to play music."

Like Vic, Mike Swiatlowski notes that the party atmosphere doesn't have to mean getting drunk or high. "They're kind of like these little parties where you have this social circle, but you feel like you're doing something and are so much involved; it's not a passive entertainment," he says about shows he booked at Old Store and then the Shed. "I've seen great bands in big clubs. The sound quality is amazing but it's never got me in the same way as when I've helped set this up or my buddies helped set this up or that's my friend's band playing. There's a lot of pride in this stuff."

If the BYOB space can feel too loose, more about hanging out than actually seeing bands and being part of a punk community, there was certainly a time when the sober space was equally problematic. The common "No booze, no drugs, no jerks" mantra (and it's various spin-offs) emerges from a vision of punk rock grounded in radical politics and community connection. But in practice some of the sober spaces enacted the no booze and no drugs portion of this slogan while lacking concern about the "no jerks" part. Both Kim Nolan and Calbee Mundy spoke highly of the important influence of Club Blitz on their personal connections to a straight edge scene, a place where they made new friends and were able to engage with a less destructive form of punk. At the same time, Calbee is able to re-read that scene through the eyes of someone who is older and has more experience with more diverse forms of punk (both the music and the scenes). "If you would have come in there with booze or drugs, you probably would have got your ass kicked. It was the start of New York hardcore where there was zero tolerance for any of that. And most of the dudes were eighteen, sober, and full of testosterone so they wanted to fight people for anything."

The ghosts of those militaristic approaches to policing punk through straight edge dogma can re-appear in some scenes, but in general there was a clear break that happened in the early 1990s that started to find its feet as the decade advanced. Punks became interested in a more expansive vision of punk that harkened back to the spectrum of sounds that tended to feature prior to the shift from punk to hardcore. This broadened sonic landscape both reflected and developed alongside an incorporation of feminism, a greater concern among some punks about a lack of racial diversity, and efforts to challenge heterosexism in the scene. Once again, DIY spaces became places where these ideas could be lived.

Peeple Watchin', 08/08/13, Fort Warner, Somerville MA

"I learned, he learned, we all learned"

I'm chatting with my friend Lou about shows we have seen together in the past few years. It's been a while since our schedules have aligned, but tonight has worked out well and we've been able to meet up at a space called Old Mount Happy that opened a few months back in Chicago's Pilsen neighborhood. The bill is really good, featuring two excellent touring bands from Philadelphia (The Stasi and The Holidays) plus a nice mix of local punk bands (Broken Prayer, Crude Humor, and Sputter). Almost all of the shows Lou and I attended together were at spaces that no longer exist. Some were probably expected to last longer. For example, Bread and Butter was an old storefront that was used for one show. Rumors within the scene suggested that this space was rented to host shows and the landlord was supposedly aware, but I can't say where the truth lies since I have never seen the guy again who was living in that space. Bread and Butter's location in a more middle-class residential neighborhood seemed to me like a potential problem for creating and maintaining a viable space, so perhaps the landlord was absentee or maybe the renter was unrealistic about the noise. Other shows Lou and I saw together happened at one-off locales (e.g., a rock lotto show to raise money for CLITFest 2013 at an art space also in Pilsen and a little northeast of here).

We scan this place, assessing its potential lifespan. There are some features that work in favor of longevity. Most notably, Old Mount Happy is the basement of a storefront that is surrounded by businesses that are closed at night. The lone business open this late is a mini-mart that will certainly benefit from Old Mount Happy being a BYOB spot. The other major land use in the area is a park across the street, which is going to be empty when shows are happening. One would assume that the apartments above this storefront are far enough up from the basement that the sound won't travel. If folks hear anything at all, they might assume the faint sounds are from a stereo playing in a nearby apartment. Also, the space is large and meets a variety of needs for DIY shows: enough room for bands to set up at the far northern end, sufficient width so punks can mosh and so others can avoid being bumped into by moshers, alcoves where band equipment can be stored, and ample length so bands and distros can set up

merch tables near the entrance to the basement and far enough away from space where the bands play and the dancers slam.

But then I consider the space from a pessimistic standpoint, looking for reasons that another potentially good spot will likely fail. This basement is a bit of a mess. There is a steady flow of dust coming from somewhere (enough that when I get home and hop into the shower, black snot flows from my nose). Metal pipes are strewn about on the floor along the western wall. Looking around this room, people smoking cigarettes in the basement, a table set up to sell beer and shots, a guy hacking after taking a hit of weed from his pipe, the use of this space seems to work to undo the locational benefits. Then the lights go out. The basement is pitch black. Someone screeches. The lights come back on. A guy is messing with the power box, which is partially dislodged from the eastern wall. Somehow between the end of a really cool set from The Holidays (which is one guy singing and playing a guitar and perhaps running some kind of sampler) and The Stasi setting up to play, the outlets have shorted out. The Stasi aren't getting any sound from their instruments or the PA, and the lights at that end of the basement are not working. There are lights that work near the basement steps. But then the basement blacks out again as some guys flip the switches on the power box. I notice that the guys who are trying to find a solution to the electricity problems are the members of The Stasi, a touring band from Philadelphia. It's their first time in this space. The Chicago punks who should know how to solve this problem seem more interested in smoking cigarettes, choking on weed, and running their beer table.

The Stasi finally play their set after someone runs a very long orange extension cord down the stairs, along the western wall of the basement, and up to the north end where the band is set up. People in attendance are really into the band; however, the experience of a touring band having to solve electrical problems provides a window into the world of a relationship between touring and hospitality. If we unpack what it means to be a host, a series of issues start to come into focus. Promoters should be feeding bands and collecting money at the door so bands can be properly paid—locals shouldn't be haggling over donations—and bands have a responsibility to respond to people in local scenes with an openness and appreciation.

The word "community" is thrown around a lot. Often the term is strategically empty when used in public discourse. For example, we regularly hear or read statements like: "The Boston community is concerned about state cuts to local public school budgets." Such phrasing portrays an imagined "we" in an effort to advance an agenda or to help foster support from people who might see themselves in that grouping even if those individuals have never had contact with one another and probably will not in the future. Because the term "community" is considered positive, incorporating the word into arguments for or against some action or belief can be effective. We might identify specific types of communities that are problematic (e.g., people who gather together for dog fighting), but we are not going to condemn community itself. I am guessing most people have not encountered arguments for the elimination of community. The term "community" would fit into the rhetorician Richard Weaver's category of a god term (i.e., a term that is particularly vague, but has a great deal of power). Thus, most of the problematically slippery uses of the term "community" lead to little analysis. Sticking with the example above about the so-called Boston community, critically informed reactions are likely to focus on school funding, not the use of the term "community." Any media outlet that reports on cuts to education funding is not going to receive emails or calls from audience members

who are upset about the misuse of "community." Instead, audience members will agree or disagree with the allocation of public school funds or about some perceived political bias in the reporting. A clear sign that one is engaged in some type of community effort is a very explicit meta-discussion about community itself. Members in a true community are interested in defining the community and will discuss how the community is enacted, sustained, and changing in various positive or negative ways. Discourse about community has been and remains a central feature of punk culture. Punks are deeply concerned with the ways that punk is lived together, including calling out groups or individuals who seem to undermine the community.

Show spaces are also sites to do community and locations to consider the possibilities for and limits to connections among punks. For example, Ana Armengod explains to me that she regularly sees bands at other houses in Columbus, Ohio even though she lives at Legion of Doom. "To me it's really important to have that. To be able to create a community in which you open yourself to see other bands, to other experiences, you have to support other houses." Sociologist Herman Schmalenbach wrote in the edited collection, *Theories of Society*, that "we cannot purposely act to create community." Instead, he notes that community emerges organically; it "develops on the basis of natural interdependence." But Ana's comment highlights the ways that the practice of community might be more complicated than Schmalenbach pronounced. She describes how community can be constructed through the actions of its members. Developing community connections takes effort and there is often some kind of reflection related to individual and collective actions.

In the face of increasing reliance on media technologies for communication with friends and family members that can feel abstract and disembodied, the intimacy of the DIY punk show provides an opportunity to reconsider how people share experiences in a physical space. Chuck Coffey, who has played in various bands based in Boulder and Denver, Colorado, explains to me that most of the shows in the early-to-mid 2000s in the Denver scene embodied the kind of spirit that helps sustain community. "If you were doing some kind of underground music, people were supportive whether they liked your band or not. In my circle of friends we refer to it a lot as 'friendcore.' You don't give a shit what the bands sound like [in terms of sub-genre of punk]." Instead, bands are booked on a bill or invited on a tour because of the quality of the relationships. The scene is more important than the sound, although there are going to be sounds that some people dig more than others.

In a *HeartattaCk* 35 interview, Ceylon from the band Pezz argues that "a sense of community is creeping across the country despite the further commodification of the underground." Ceylon claims that community is "built up and strengthened in ways that I didn't see coming years ago." He describes something national in focus, but more often than not it's the local connections where punks feel as if they are in community. In part, these connections happen because local spaces provide a site for physical connections. "There's a special kind of community that has come from it being a clubhouse for weirdoes and fuckups for nearly three decades," says Ray Martinez from the band Autonomy about Lost Cross during a May 2013 *MRR* interview. Nikki from Autonomy adds: "If my mom hadn't dropped me off for shows at Lost Cross when I was twelve years old, my life would probably not have been the same. I don't know if that is good or bad, but that gross house has had a lot do with who I am."

Some punks might feel as if they are members of a community more generally. Others may consider engaging with like-minded people at DIY shows to be an enactment of community. Another group will consider DIY shows to be opportunities to hang out with friends or acquaintances. And there will certainly be a collection of people who go to shows because punk offers possibilities even though this group feels alienated within a scene that promises egalitarianism but replicates racist, sexist, and heterosexist mainstream norms. Chuck's phrasing of "friendcore" seems to account for the first three types of social relationships within a scene. At the same time, the term "friendcore" also provides a more humorous description of group connections that can circumvent the lofty expectations that accompany identifying a collection of people as a community.

"It's debatable whether a 'punk community' exists," writes Jessica Skolnik in a guest column in the October 2011 issue of *MRR*. "I personally find it more useful to take it as a given that the social connections and relationships formed by our overlapping interests and experiences constitute some kind of community and instead ask what that community looks like (from varying perspectives, because it sure as hell ain't a monolith) and what we'd like it to look like." Jessica has been involved with an effort to start a volunteer-run DIY space in Chicago, so she's clearly tuned in to the important relationship between show spaces and social connections through punk, but she raises a crucial point about expecting too much when punk rock is described as community. Punk is made up of varied sounds and a heterogeneous mixture of people. Therefore, one might think about community through close and personal relationships, some of which are ongoing (e.g., people who live in a town and see each other at shows and hang out socially), and then there are punks who perhaps tour regularly and have bonded with people in that same town. But those relationships exist irregularly in person and tend to be maintained via various media (Facebook, texting, Twitter). These bands, promoters, and members of scenes would still identify as one even if the physical time together is limited.

Jessica's comment also can be applied to the various ways that house shows will reflect some vision among people at that house about the role of community. Nevin Marshall explains to me that a BYOB house can limit how people interact. "But the show itself, by not [allowing] drinking, created more community because everybody could have a conversation and it wasn't about a ripping, raw party, which doesn't create community. It's fun

but it doesn't create community. If we can talk to each other and hang out, I think that creates more of a community." Nevin explains that he understands how the social interactions that happen while people drink can be fun and can extend from bonds formed among people in the scene, but his point about BYOB spaces is that the party becomes more important than the cultural politics, which means the conversation will likely shift in tone.

To consider Jessica's question about what community should or could look like in the context of DIY show spaces, let's start with the ways that a promoter and other members of a scene foster a welcoming environment for locals (both regulars and people who are finding their way into punk) and for touring bands. "The whole aspect of letting people into your living space. You are essentially opening your door to strangers," Al Pist tells me. "If you are a band that is unknown, who is not going to get guarantees or maybe even get paid that night, if you didn't have that hospitality there's no way a lot of bands could tour." Al's discussion of hospitality reflects a key component of ways that community can be enacted while avoiding the kind of unrealistic monolithic model that Jessica critiques.

The people I interviewed repeatedly stressed the importance of hospitality. For some, like Chuck, that openness stretched from show promoters to the local scene more generally. "I think that Denver is very hospitable to touring bands. Bands would come and we'd make friends, trade shows. That happens in other places, but it's not like some of the bigger cities where you have to go [to a house] two or three times to make a friend versus other places where you don't know anybody but by the end of the night you've got a place to stay with someone who is gonna be a friend for the next fifteen years. I really think that Denver is one of those kinds of towns."

E. E. Evans-Pritchard writes in the introduction to Marcel Mauss' book, *The Gift*, that Mauss offers an alternative model for considering social relationships. "Mauss is telling us, quite pointedly," Prichard argues, "how much we have lost, whatever we may have otherwise gained, by substitution of a rational economic system for a system in which exchange of goods was not a mechanical but a moral transaction, bringing about and maintaining human, personal, relationships between individuals and groups." Mauss' description of a gift economy provides a framework to understand the kind of relationships that develop among punks involved with show spaces and in touring bands. "We've really enjoyed the opportunities and experience of traveling around the country, playing music, and we try to plan trips whenever time allows," says Luke from Sinaloa in a *HeartattaCk* issue 48 interview with Katy Otto. "We've met so many good people over the last few years, all over the country, and owe many, many people for their hospitality."

Money is not the inspiration for DIY touring. Nor is getting paid the foundation for the social relationships that form during tours. Kent McClard describes in his June 1994 *MRR* column how this gift economy takes shape in a DIY touring context: "Punk rock is about doing things you love. Punk rock is about getting in a band and traveling around the country and meeting new people and building foundations and knowing that these new friends aren't after your money or your fame or your image." Although there are some people who view DIY as an entry point into fame and mini-fortunes, and the quantity of people who felt this might have been larger in the early 1990s, most people involved with DIY punk are motivated by social and aesthetic experiences. These goals animate the choices of local show promoters and touring bands.

In fact, there is something ironic about the work that goes into doing shows that highlights a community focus in punk. "If I tried out for a job for event planning or something [laughs],

I don't even know if I would get it," James Payne says to me. "And it's what I have been doing for a decade in all sorts of conditions. I've been curating for a decade, as I define it. It's kind of bizarre but if there is no career objective then it's much more pure. Everyone there wants to be there. People like each other generally. You're building a shared set of values and a shared aesthetic."

Al Pist helps us see the extent to which Kent McClard is right about DIY touring in that punks not only lack mainstream goals and interests but they are guided by an understanding of the struggles with touring. Again, Al claims that there was never an explicit conversation among members of The Pist that they would host shows once they moved into a house together. Instead, the band "wanted to reciprocate for all the times that people had put us up and helped us out with shows." Al and his bandmates "knew what it was like to be on tour and not have a place to play or stay."

Martin Sorrondeguy notes in a June 1994 *HeartattaCk* interview that he witnessed a positive transformation in the punk scene tied to house shows. "The whole basement show scene" was an effort to break away from "big corporate punk," Martin argues. "So it was kind of like out of desperation for punks who were really into it as a movement to do that. They had to break away." The communication improved, he observes, which facilitates this DIY alternative. "I think the things that are going on now, and the bands that have been around in the past five years have been fucking incredible and have all played a really important part in the survival of this movement and creating it into a totally different level than what it was." He explains that most of the hardcore bands that came through Chicago in the late 1980s were playing clubs, which affected how punks related to one another. "When we go on tour we're playing basement shows which I love more than anything. Because there's no better way of being intimate with the crowd than in a basement show. It's just...you're there, you're engulfed in each other. You're up in each other's faces and you're sharing yourself with people and it's the best thing that can be happening. That never existed before, at least not around here [Chicago]."

Martin describes how this approach to working together is tied to a political economy as well as experiential opportunities. The intimacy that is crucial to the house show experience is also a key component to punk community, as Martin implies when distinguishing between corporate and DIY approaches to punk. However, the positive description of this experience by Martin is unfortunately balanced from time-to-time with a variety of shows that lack the social connections that should be central features of any DIY show.

After Nevin and his friends moved out of the Hoople Mansion in Fort Myers, Florida, the house continued as a show space. "There's been two sets of punk kids since us, both of which have been largely disasters," Nevin tells me. The first group was not good for the scene because they were interested in a more "nihilistic" approach to punk, claims Nevin: heroin use and "sketchy dudes" showing up carrying guns and bringing prostitutes to shows. "The new group that is there has good intentions but they just don't get it." Nevin explains that he offered advice about running shows, but stressed that he had no intention of taking over their shows. For Nevin, well-run shows are especially important given the reputation Fort Myers has built based on quality show promotion dating back to the 1990s. This new generation of kids in Hoople Mansion seemed to understand Nevin's point. "And they'd say, 'Oh, yeah. I screwed up. I get it. This time we're going to man the door and we're gonna cook for the band,'" Nevin tells me with a tone of optimism (as if reliving the conversations). "And so the next band would come and I would call up, 'Hey, do you need me to make food for them?' And he'd say, 'Nah, I got it.' After the show the band came back to my house because I said I'd host them and they asked, 'Do you mind if we cook some pasta here?' And I asked if he fed them. 'No, we were playing Frisbee and he asked if we were hungry. We said, "Yeah." He said he'd go in and cook and he never did.' Are you kidding me! I offered to do it myself and he said he's got it. That level of irresponsibility or not following through..." Nevin trails off with an exasperated tone. Optimism gives way to deflation in a matter of seconds.

Dan Dittmer tells me that he regularly heard through the grapevine that Rapid City, South Dakota was a favorite destination for bands to play. Much of this had to do with the local kids responding positively to touring bands. However, that chatter among bands about the Rapid City scene was certainly linked to Dan's overall approach to promoting shows, which included being a good host. He understood that touring bands were not going to make much money from the shows given the population size in Rapid City, so he prioritized a communal experience. "When you're on the road and somebody's like, 'Dude, I'm making the food, you go take a shower and wash your clothes' and tomorrow morning they will have a full belly, clean clothes, and be back on the road then that word started spreading," he says.

Perhaps the kids in Nevin's scene who ask about meals and then don't follow through are more of the norm than Dan, if one charts the recurring discussion in zines about feeding bands. A letter from Andre Preuss to *MRR* in the June 2006 issue focuses more directly on this issue of food. Andre finds claims that people can't feed bands to be "rather silly," adding that providing a meal for touring bands seems to be common practice everywhere except in the U.S. "Yes, putting on a show involves finding a place to hold the show, finding places to stay for the bands (which isn't that common in the U.S. either, I'm told), making flyers and posters and putting them up and so on. But most of this should be done way in advance." He notes that the only thing that should concern the promoter on the actual day of the show is preparing food and having phone numbers for friends who could help out in case of some kind of emergency. While I agree with Andre's assessment more generally, it is important to remember the context of most house shows. Punks in their late teens or early twenties book the bulk of these shows. Although there are certainly members of this population who have culinary skills and make healthy food choices, many are living on steady diet of fast food, frozen food, or preservatives masquerading as food. If these punks aren't cooking for themselves, they can't magically transform into chefs on the few days each month that bands are hosted. Moreover, most promoters are either working service industry jobs on hourly wages or are enrolled in school full time. Thus, many of these punks are working the day of the show. The time it takes to make a meal after arriving home from these other commitments might prohibit such features of hosting.

None of this is meant to let local punks off the hook. Again, if a scene is built on a belief that some type of punk community is the goal and hospitality is one of the central ways that community is enacted in a scene, then the promoter needs to extend her or his network. Those people in the scene who function as the emergency backups that Andre mentions might also help with the shows in some capacity. Friends could cook for the bands, people could collect money at the door, others might know what to do with the soundboard, and maybe someone will know what to do when the electricity is not working. Instead of relying on the promoter to do everything, punks should be working cooperatively to host touring bands. Those efforts will have an added benefit of modeling for local kids in the scene what it means to do it together.

Moreover, taking care of meals and sleeping arrangements can help make up for a smaller crowd or a show that lacks energy for one reason or another. "The first time I toured Europe was 2004 or 2005 and that completely changed the way I do shows. The first show I played there, there was a spread of food for the bands, a cool place to sleep, there was food in the morning," Chris Moore explains to me. "The promoter took care of the band. Even though no one even knew who the fuck we were, it was the same treatment for everybody. I always do that now. My theory is that if the food is really good and the show sucks, it's less of a blow. I always try to make the best food I possibly can."

Hospitality extends beyond making sure bands are fed. The decision to promote a show comes with other responsibilities, such as understanding the finances of touring. There are a variety of methods punks use to collect money for a touring band. The best approach is to have someone standing at the door to the space where people enter to see the bands play. Such a move insures that anyone who wants to enter is asked to donate money for the touring band(s). Some promoters don't like to do this because they want to model an anti-capitalist approach to doing shows. Others seem to be disorganized or inexperienced and don't think about the spatial dynamics that make standing at the door an effective move.

A second technique adopted by promoters is to walk around the space and ask each person to donate. Some people are very polite about this and others understand that being courteous must sometimes be tempered with a more aggressive method. "I had this pumpkin that I would walk around with and I would say, 'Give me your money! Donate,'" Jenny Ray tells me about collecting money at the Bike House. "I feel that a majority of the people were there to support the bands and check them out and donate their money to 'em." But this move can be less effective if the promoter or one of her or his friends is less assertive. Bull Gervasi tells me that looking back at the second Policy of 3 tour still leaves him confused about how the band actually did the tour. "That was at a point where our LP had come out and we were starting to get a little better known so more people were coming out to see us," he claims. This tour was an improvement over the first one because more of the shows were better organized, but at this point in the mid-1990s, better organized is relative. "I have a lot of the notes that I took during those tours (We played in Minneapolis at this space and we sold this many records, this many T-shirts, and were paid this much). Just looking back at some of those notes it kind of blows my mind: 'Got paid $14.55, sold three 7"s.' It's like, 'Jesus Christ, how did we ever manage to make it around the country?' Luckily gas was a lot cheaper in those days, but we sure as hell barely got paid anything."

Gas prices have gone up and some of the problems experienced by bands in the past continue in the present. "We've played shows where the donation bucket thing does not work," Jim Gies says about Boilerman tours. "We played a show in Minneapolis where there were at least twenty or twenty-five people there. Not a huge show, but enough, and the dude gave us, and I quote, '$9 and a little bit of weed.' And I was like, 'Well, none of us smoke weed and $9 is not super good.'" Cam Myers recalls that when he was booking shows at FSU Garage they always collected money at the door, but now he lives in Minneapolis, where he has observed an approach that shows how Boilerman's experience there is sadly more of a norm than an anomaly. "Here they do a lot of pass around the bucket, which is kind of bogus for the bands. A couple guys here get a bad rap: 'So and so is doing the show and he always makes everyone pay' sort of thing. The people that are complaining are the people who don't care about the music." Jim adds that whenever they play Cincinnati, "usually it's donation buckets and it goes fine. I think it's what the scene is like and what kind of expectations are clear. I can't put a cigarette or beer in the gas tank."

There is a fine line between temporary ignorance grounded in a true lack of understanding and sustained ignorance connected to an inability to consider the experiences of other people. Alexander Lesher explains that some of his early choices were all wrong when it came to organizing a show. He acknowledges that he lacked role models (both people and experiences at other house shows) when he was starting out. "My attitude evolved over the years as soon as I started to play out," he tells me. "I would get irritated by the way in which it was put together," Alexander says in reference to shows he would play. "I'd think, 'Why? I can't do this to other people.'"

Because there is very little mentoring that happens, going on the road helps punks learn what it means to be paid based on someone standing at the door, to be fed a meal, and offered a place to sleep. Jordan Brand explains to me that he wasn't really mentored at all, but he learned a lot by talking with touring bands that came through Omaha, Nebraska for shows he booked.

Many promoters also need to learn how to navigate a range of excuses from people who arrive without money. The percentage of punks who claim that they don't have the funds to pay a donation seems to be small, but punks showing up without money (often with beer in hand) is steady enough that almost everyone I interviewed who books shows in a BYOB space had multiple stories about this problem. Jim explains how he handles the situation: "When people tell me they don't have money, I will ask: 'You don't even have a dollar?' And if they come in with other people, I will ask, 'Can this person lend you money?' I won't turn people away but I make it clear that this is not free to do, so people shouldn't just be free to stroll in."

Cam Myers links this recurring problem of not wanting to pay for a show to a larger problem with a lack of thoughtfulness in the scene. "One big thing I think about that I don't think most people think about is just how much effort and how thankless it is to run a DIY space," he explains. "Even to book shows, most of those people don't get the appreciation that the band playing does. They're hustling: making flyers and trying to promote stuff. There are people that might know, but the majority don't. I always try to say thanks or give them a beer if I know they drink, 'cause here [Minneapolis] a lot of people are like, 'I don't have any money, can I come in?' and the promoters have to deal with that bullshit."

A promoter can be well organized when it comes to hosting bands, making sure local punks have received flyers and information via social media, money will be collected to support the touring band, the bands will be fed, and the touring band has a place to sleep; however, hospitality extends to the scene more generally and sometimes local punks don't do their part. Brian Chamblee who books shows in Austin, Texas and plays in two different bands that tour a lot (Chest Pain and For Want Of), tells me that problems with hosting DIY house shows in Austin are almost always tied to money. "One of the first shows I did I had some major troubles with the people. There were probably seventy people at the show. And only ten came in because they refused to pay the $5 entrance fee. I was like, 'Well, it's $5. You can hang out in the front yard and listen to the bands from outside the house or you can pay the $5 and come in,'" he remembers. "The majority decided to stay outside and not pay. The touring band was about to play and they said, 'Hey, we'd rather play to a whole bunch of people that aren't going to pay to watch us than not have anyone watch us.' They asked me to let everyone come in and I told them, 'You're not going to get paid any more' and they said, 'That's alright.'"" Brian explains that Austin is a strange scene because free shows are the norm in that city. "To get people to understand the idea, 'Hey, you have to pay because these bands are spending a lot of money on gas' wasn't exactly easy."

It's important to note the ways that punks respond to such requests to pay. In Austin, punks didn't want to pay but how they reacted to the door charge was likely filtered through Brian's race and gender. Nicole Pagowsky explains to me that she experienced similar resistance at shows she had booked at her house, The Owl Sanctuary, in Madison, Wisconsin, but wonders aloud if reactions to her requests for money were also imbued with a negative reaction to her identity. "I collected money at the door. I was very serious about that and I would get called a bitch all the time," Nicole says laughing. "'These people are traveling from pretty far away. If you can afford to buy a 30-pack of beer, you can afford to pay,'" she remembers telling people who did not want to donate. "It was interesting to think if the same problem would have happened if I was a guy. Would I have been called a bitch?" Beyond these fools, though, people in Madison seemed to understand what was happening, unlike punks who attended the first few shows Brian organized.

But Brian stuck with the approach of asking for a donation, because he knew this was the right thing to do, and eventually local punks would get it. He claims that any show at Slamalot, which was the name of Brian's house at that time, would have a $5 donation. "I always kept it $5 whether the band was coming from out of the country or coming from San Antonio an hour away. That way people were gonna know that this is how much they pay every time they come to my house. It took a couple shows but eventually I didn't have to ask; people already had their money out and would pay."

In effect, Brian had to teach the local punks what it meant to host touring bands, to develop a hospitable scene. Punk rock pedagogy is interesting to me for a few reasons. First, learning contexts can inspire all who are involved. I learn as much from my students as they hopefully learn from me. Second, punks who hope to enact a vision of punk grounded in community should strive to learn from one another (how to make zines, how to put on shows, how to distribute records). Finally, community is not static, nor should it be. The best way to improve one's community (whatever "best" means in the context of a specific community) is to be open to dialogue and debate, which will affirm the features of one's community that are positive and offer models to change those features of one's community that might be problematic in some way. I often wonder if the "yourself" in DIY leads people to miss out on shared efforts to work within one's scene. With this in mind, Nevin's offer to help a newer generation of punks in the Hoople Mansion stands out as one way that community can be fostered and hospitality modeled.

Mickie Rat notes that he knew what to do when he first started hosting shows at Casa de Chaos because he had been exposed to show production and promotion through a number of experiences, beginning when he was a young kid. Mickie's dad worked at Universal Amphitheater, a well-known concert venue in Southern California that hosts large touring bands (e.g., Elvis Costello, Dwight Yoakam, Burning Spear). Mickie spent his summers hanging out there when he was a kid and learned through conversations and observation about the positive features of working with people who have their shit together and the ways that the same job can be miserable when people are flaky. Later on, when he formed his own band, which was prior to moving into Casa, he developed relationships with local promoters. "There were three different local promoters and two of them became my friends. They kind of took me under their wing and said, 'You're in a band and you want a show? Here's how to promote a show.' And they would take me with them to make flyers and to hand out flyers. So I learned what they were doing just by hanging out with them. By '92 I knew the basics of running a show because I would help them work the door at shows or help them stage-manage at shows."

"Stepping back a bit, one of the things I'm most proud of is that I kind of taught other people to do it," he says. "It shouldn't be one person running things all the time; it should be a bunch of people pitching in, which was my ultimate goal. Anybody could run a show at any time without everybody being there."

The larger message of punk ("You can do this too") is both its blessing and its curse, which is evidenced in the ways that the same successes and same failures with show promotion and production repeat over time. For example, I asked Bull if he noticed major changes when comparing his first tour with Policy of 3 in 1993 to the time R.A.M.B.O. broke up in 2007. "Not entirely. But that's kind of the thing with punk; it's one of the few places where someone can go from being a spectator to being an active participant pretty quick. They can decide: 'I'm going to start doing shows in my living room. I don't know what I'm fuckin' doing, but I like this band and I've seen other people do it.'

Jordan Brand adds that there is another downside to the lack of mentoring that happens with booking shows. He argues that when a kid rents an expensive space that is nicer than normally used and/or agrees to pay a $500 guarantee because mom and dad gave the kid the money, or when a large bonus at work can be used to pay for the space or band, that bands develop a skewed sense of what's possible within a scene. Jordan notes that Omaha, Nebraska wasn't big enough to sustain such mistakes. Bands started demanding what they received in the past even though those kids who had footed the bill were no longer around.

There have been various tools over the years that deal with show promotion. For example, *Book Your Own Fuckin' Life* provided a model for working together and sharing DIY resources. But the zine did not take people through the steps of booking, promoting, and running shows. Other zines and Internet sites have offered more direct instruction, but the ephemeral nature of these resources means that today's guides are tomorrow's recycle bin materials and rotten links. Bands also must figure out how to do DIY. Of course, there is no one way to book a show or to tour. A cookie-cutter approach would certainly be antithetical to punk's chaotic spirit, and the desire to avoid unified methods seems to reaffirm that punk community is not a singular way of being together. But this desire to be different can sometimes hinder how hospitality is enacted and community is maintained.

That first band that asked Brian to let everyone into the house who refused to pay faced one of the recurring tensions that takes shape in the punk scene and is not applicable in other live music contexts. Mainstream venues that cater to other genres of music draw people who expect to pay money to see the bands. Reggae fans, rap fans, and rock fans don't show up to a venue expecting to get in for free. Although there are some artists working in each of those genres who raise questions about problems with capitalism, punk is one of the few genres of music grounded in a desire to radically re-think the rules of music production and consumption, which includes how tours and local shows are organized.

In an anonymous letter to *MRR* in the April 2011 issue, the writer responded to a column written by Mariam Bastani about punk bands playing corporate events. The letter writer notes,

"We came home from this last tour (where we played the Scion garage fest) completely broke, jobless, hungry, and those in the band who did not have help from loved ones to get by essentially became hobos. It took several months to get back to being able to live in a semi-stable lifestyle. Without taking money from companies like Scion, the lifestyle I mentioned earlier would have been impossible. I reiterate. It would have been impossible to live like SHIT without their money. You are not only attacking my integrity but my desire to play music and eat food on the same day." Mariam's response followed. She argued that the anonymous writer failed to see the available possibilities when punk bands tour. "If you belong to a DIY community, garage, punk or otherwise, and claim that you cannot tour or make music without corporate sponsorship, that is a flat out lie," she claims. "For years and years various types of music based in DIY ethics have existed without corporate sponsorship." Finally, she remarks, in response to the letter writer's assertion that the band eats horrible fast food when touring because that's all they can afford: "Each band I have been in has toured extensively and we have managed to remain healthy, not eat shitty fast food, have jobs, and even bring kids on tour on working class wages."

I noted in previous chapters that there is a kind of professionalism required when hosting shows. I understand

that such phrasing runs counter to the spirit of amateurism that is central to punk's ethos. There are problematic practices associated with professionalism, most notably treating people as means to some financial end rather than members of some collective or communal effort to create and experience alternative ways of being together and making music. Mariam describes making the right political choices, which can guide bands in ways that reflect a kind of professionalism (including what people eat and how they organize their shows to play DIY spaces). "Being more professional when it comes to doing shows does not mean you are less DIY. DIY should be better than main stream," says Ryan Cappelletti from Punks Before Profits Records in letter to *MRR* in April 2006. "We should be able to offer people more not less. We offer community—the corporate shit houses that do shows can't offer that."

Those choices to do things the right way can influence the experiences that punks have in their local scenes and on the road. Again, Chuck's comment about "friendcore" highlights that punk community is very much about the experience of personal connections and that there are a number of ways that such relationships can develop. For example, Mike Swiatlowski tells me, "Passing out flyers was a great way to meet other people and led to a lot of the personal relationships." This vision of "friendcore" also relates to relationships among bands on tour. Bull fondly remembers Policy of 3 playing a house show in North Carolina with Groundwork, Sparkmarker, and Undertow. "So it was four touring bands, none of whom were particularly popular at the time, but we all had a really great time seeing each other, meeting each other, hanging out. We all went swimming together afterwards."

Hospitality is ultimately grounded in a mutual connection. Promoters and members of a local scene should be taking care of bands, but the bands have a responsibility to understand what's involved for a promoter who is hosting a show. John Boilard explains to me that he was able to host shows at The Shed for a long time because his efforts were matched by the commitments of the bands to not only playing exciting music but also interacting with people at the show, including his mom. "People wouldn't be outside talking; they'd be inside chatting with her and the bands would say, 'Your mom's the best ever. I just had a half-hour conversation with her and she told me the funniest story about you.' She was diggin' it. She made friends. There would be people that would come regularly and just hang out in the kitchen with my mom. As far as staying in the house, they realize that this is a place to play but also someone's home, someone's mom's house. They were sweet as pie. They could be the weirdest, aggressive, wigged out people but as soon as they step in the door they're like, 'Ma'am this is great.'"

But not all bands meet hospitality with appreciation. Al Pist tells me, "One day I came home from work and there were four crusty looking dudes in my living room that I had never seen before in my life. As I walked in the living room, I saw that the couch cushion was on fire and one of the guys was pouring a beer on it. I didn't even acknowledge them. I just walked right upstairs and asked my roommates, 'Who the fuck is this?'" He notices, though, that most of the problems aren't from the "lifers." Instead, "it's the people who are punks for the summer" who treat punk as a phase in their life, a brief time for rebellion before they focus their efforts on more normative aspirations: finding a career, getting married, buying a house, having kids, identifying the right retirement plan. "The punks who still go to shows are the ones who were respectful or if they saw something going on, they would try to stop it or pitch in to help clean up after the show."

Ana notes that there aren't many problems with local punks in Columbus, but there are issues with touring bands here and there. "Sadly there's been bands that we're not comfortable with," she says. Although the people who book Legion of Doom obviously can identity bands that don't fit with the general politics of the house, it's hard to know about interpersonal relationships until the band arrives to play. She adds that the politics of the house also influence whether or not bands want to sleep there. "Being that the Legion of Doom is a sober space some bands feel like the three hours that they were here and couldn't drink was enough."

I think back to Cam's claim that booking shows can be a thankless experience. He is not suggesting that people say to promoters: "Oh, I'm so happy that you exist." Rather, it's important that punks understand that some people—the people who book shows or open up their houses for punk shows—do a lot of work to make a scene materialize. Those efforts are key inspirations for writing this book. Punk as a genre of music has excited me from the time I was a little kid. The ideas expressed in the lyrics and the sounds created by the bands have resonated for me since I first heard the Ramones' *Road to Ruin*, but materially being able to gather together in a space is how the community happens, how politics are discussed and debated, it gives the bands a space to play. Without these spaces, punk is a radically different culture. Those of us who go to house shows probably know that seeing shows in a bar or in a club is just not the same. People start to take the spaces for granted after a while. "Oh, yeah, there's gonna be a show here." And then what happens when that space doesn't exist anymore? Will someone else do the work that

Spitboy, 4/9/94 Cabbage Collective Show, Calvary Church, West Philadelphia

needs to be done to create a show space? Or will people sit back and wait for someone else to do it, focusing on the "yourself" in DIY instead of considering the ways that DIY is really about ourselves, the collective, a community? Each member of a scene needs to work to help make a hospitable scene that welcomes touring bands, that helps produce safe spaces for locals, and that displays appropriate gratitude for the promoters who work hard to do shows in the right way.

People in Your Neighborhood

In early 2013 the underground was buzzing as word spread throughout the U.S. that Boston police officers created various fake social media accounts in an attempt to find and then bust DIY shows. When I first heard about this, I assumed the police were acting in a fashion that mirrored what has been happening since punks started doing DIY shows in the late 1970s and early 1980s. Cops break up shows all the time. They hear the music while patrolling or receive complaints from neighbors who are worried about noise, people milling about on the sidewalk or in alleys, or scruffy looking people engaging in suspicious activities such as moving things in and out of vans. Given this track record of busting shows, there doesn't appear to be a need to infiltrate a scene for the purposes of shutting down a show. Most reasonable people who have experiences with punk shows know this, so it seemed to me that all of the uproar in the scene was a twisted sense of self-importance among punks who love to engage a variety of real and imagined foes. But then more information began to circulate about emails and Facebook messages phrased in the exact same way sent to a variety of DIY promoters. These messages were loaded with behind-the-times slang as senders worked really hard to establish street cred.

"I've gotten on my personal Facebook account friend requests from, I want to say, a dozen or more fake profiles that were only friend requesting me for purposes of trying to figure out where a DIY show was," Zach Weeks explains to me. "You can just tell that there is something wrong; they're not spam accounts and they're also not joke accounts." Zach's experiences were mirrored by multiple promoters in Boston. Luke O'Neil describes in a *Slate* article, "Boston Punk Zombies Are Watching You," how Facebook messages from Donna Giordano as well as e-mails from Joe Sly (whose email address "bostonbeatgang" linked to the name of a former hardcore gang) were sent to local promoters and touring bands coming to Boston. After reading O'Neil's article Liz Pelly went back through old email and Facebook inboxes and found the same messages sent to her that other promoters received and on the same dates. Liz explained in a piece for *Stereogum* ("Boston Police Posing As Punks Online To Bust House Shows: What's The Point?") that for DIY promoters "there's a perpetual understanding that any rando emailing you for the show address could always potentially be a cop." This catfishing expedition by Boston police officers was a bit different, since their efforts appeared to be motivated by the enforcement of a Boston City Council noise ordinance that had recently passed. The ordinance was designed to eliminate so-called "public nuisances".

In a 2012 article for the *Boston Phoenix* Liz described the City Council meeting in which this public nuisance law was debated. She wrote that she had testified at that meeting about the value of house shows as an alternative to bars and clubs and had tried to explain to Council members that the concerns of most of the other citizens in attendance (all of whom supported this new measure) made sense. People urinating off balconies, partygoers vomiting on the front steps of local residences, and raging keggers happening late into the night are nuisances and residents should be pissed off about such behaviors. However, there are different types of noises that exist for different purposes. Houses used for band practices and for shows are driven by art, not by getting fucked up and then creating a public nuisance.

Zach says that three active DIY spaces in Boston were closed down after the Council unanimously passed this ordinance. The police contacted the people on the lease or went to the landlords. "Two of my friends ran a space in a loft called Trouble Ahead

Hoover, Cabbage Collective Show, Calvary Church, West Philadelphia, PA, 9/4/93

that only did shows for about six months. They got a warning that they would be evicted if they continued having shows." Tenants at another loft space were also threatened with eviction if they continued to do music-related activities, Zach explains. "They planned to have one last show. And five plain-clothes cops showed up with the guy's name who leased the space and information about him: employer, background, everything. They had him on file. They had all his band members on file. They said, 'You can't do this or we are gonna arrest you right now.'" Zach describes a scenario that would be troubling for punks, since police rarely pop up prior to a show. Although I'm sure such situations happen here and there, I have only heard about one similar situation. Joe Milik tells me that his second house in Iowa City was going to host shows, but things never got off the ground. "This is a weird situation that I've never had happen to me before or after," Joe says. "We put up flyers for the show and we had a cop come to the door the day before and say that we better not throw the show there. I guess he could have seen the flyers, but I don't know."

I think about something James Payne told me when reflecting on house shows as buffers from the police. "There's an idea that hypothetically cops can't come into your house so you really are in this private world." But James was hedging his bets with his phrasing. I assume the punks in Boston could have put up a fight and Joe could have as well, but whatever victories would have been gained in a struggle with the police would have been lost when the cops pressured landlords.

"We realized that the problem is that anything that is a source of entertainment that is somehow profiting in one way or another, even if it's miniscule, the city doesn't want it," says Zach about the Boston crackdown. "We have a lot of 'real' concert venues here. And there's a lot of colleges that also have performance/art-related things." The city is able to make money from those other venues and event spaces, so any other non-licensed space can be considered a threat to the city's tax base even though the DIY spaces don't make any money.

The Boston scenario sent shockwaves throughout the U.S. Punks began to discuss and debate locally and nationally (in person and through online forums and social media) the best tactics for avoiding police pressure. Some wrestled with the ways that certain efforts, such as finding addresses via "ask a punk," might end up closing off opportunities for people who are new to the scene. And while these tactics might help punks avoid infiltration (if such attempts even exist outside Boston), the heavy focus on one form of police pressure did not account for a variety of ways that punk houses face other strains, most notably from landlords. Because so many punks are focused on local spaces, there is little awareness of some consistent national trends that relate to the location of house spaces. Some punk houses can escape pressures form landlords and police for a while, whereas other houses are short lived. The lives of many houses could be extended if punks were more proactive about coordinating with neighbors. Unfortunately, such relationships are rarely fostered.

In Chicago three spaces closed shortly after the Boston situation was publicized. Two were related to police pressures, although it seems that only one was directly connected to the show itself. One house took a break from doing shows in the past because it was linked to neighborhood graffiti—although this time a show was shut down during a band's set. The other house was temporarily closed because an idiot was reported for urinating on a neighbor's wall or into the neighbor's basement apartment window, depending on who is telling the story. This second house is now going again, although shows are much more sporadic. The third house, Alderaan, was shut down because the landlords gave the tenants two options: remain in the house and continue to use it as a practice space, but not a show space, or leave. Alderaan's closing was conflated with the other two places and what was happening with police. Matt Walsh, one of the residents at Alderaan, explains to me what happened there: "The old tenant who used to live in the house drums and has a practice space where he saw a flyer." Apparently that guy showed the flyer and YouTube videos of shows at Alderaan to the landlords. "We communicated with the landlords as much as possible: We're gonna have parties and there's going to be music. And we said that bands would practice. But once you see a flyer that had money on it and once you see a video of people moshing in the basement, there's no, 'Oh, yeah, it was just a few friends.'"

After news about the Boston busts spread to other scenes, punks around the country shifted from putting addresses on flyers and on social media sites to an "ask a punk" approach, knowing (or hoping) that people who are involved in the scene or legitimately coming into the scene will be able to find addresses from friends or acquaintances. In Chicago, fears about police inspired the choice to stop publishing the Do It Yourself Chicago (DIYCHI) website, a resource for information about DIY-spaces and shows that provided a rare historical record of past DIY shows in the city. Matt was one of founding members of DIYCHI, a collective effort to promote shows, share information about the scene, and work toward the creation of a volunteer-run space. He notes that "the 'ask a punk' dynamic is a dangerous game." I wonder what is the role of the cops and are they really seeking it out? Or are they just trying to shut down what they view as a huge party?"

All evidence points to a unique set of problems with the police in Boston. Punks have always had to evade police, so taking a longer view of current problems can lead to more thoughtful responses by punks to police pressures. Moreover, it is important to understand how the policing of punk spaces might fit within a larger political, economic, and social context. For example, Chicago is a city with some of the worst gun violence in the country. At the time that the three Chicago houses were shut down, the mainstream news media was running with one of its favorite urban stories: wilding. A group of 15 to 200 (depending on the reports) primarily African American teens supposedly showed up on Michigan Avenue (one of the city's wealthiest shopping areas and a hub for tourists) and started beating up random people. The same problems reportedly occurred on the Chicago Transit Authority Red Line (a metro line that runs from the city's northern border down to the South Side). Are cops really worried about punk shows when this sensational violence is added to the nightly news reports about Chicago's crime rates? Anyone who pays attention to urban politics knows that the constant publicity of crime and violence is bad for tourism and could impact housing sales, which is bad for the economy, and a poor economy is the number one concern for all politicians who pressure police officials. House shows are likely a minor blip on the Chicago Police Department's radar given these other problems.

When Cold Lovers played their last show at Albion House, Carrie (the band's singer) announced that there were cops outside. The police never shut down the show. It was late at night. The basement was very crowded. It's a BYOB house where a lot of people tend to hang out in the backyard making noise. And that fog machine was spewing smoke. This would seem to be a perfect storm for cops to come in and break up a show. But they didn't.

Another example is the Coke Bust show at Coach House. Chicago PD appeared when bands were playing, but did not shut down the show. Nick Baran, who booked the show, wrote on the Facebook event page the next day that the experience "reinforced the value of not having booze at DIY punk gigs." He acknowledged that sober spaces can be a bummer for people who like to get drunk and wild, "but when the neighbors called complaining about noise, underage drinking, and trash thrown all over the neighborhood, the cops arrived to find twenty people outside and a dull roar of drums and guitar from behind the Coach House door." The police asked Nick about the reports they received regarding underage drinking and trash, since neither was visible. "I told them it was just a couple bands playing and no booze was allowed. The cop said, 'That's good. Really? No booze? Keep it down and we're good then.' And they left. It may not feel 'punk' to some but it can preserve a show from instant shutdown exactly like it did last night. So thank you to those of you who can follow some simple rules to keep shit from getting shut down."

Nick's comment about sober spaces and potential problems with the police converges with the sentiments of other punks who book sober houses. Although Nevin Marshall believes that sober spaces facilitate community connection, he also explains that shows at the Hoople Mansion were alcohol-free when he lived there because of concerns about police. If punks took out a drink, "We'd say, 'Wait until after the show, you can't have that here.' It was both for the atmosphere of the show (drunken idiots and people showing up like it was this raging, crazy party) and also because I was a teacher the whole time and I can't have young kids drinking at the house. If we get busted for noise, ok they would shut the show down. But if we get busted and there are seventeen-year-olds drinking in the house..."

Zack Furness expresses a similar concern. "That's usually the reason why places are so short-lived, you get the second or third call from the cops and you get people (who maybe are underage or who have herb on them) who don't want to deal with serious cop issues."

There's an old adage about the most important feature of real estate: location, location, location. For many people this maxim applies to identifying the best investment, but for punks the location of their houses will directly relate to problems or lack thereof with cops and landlords. The location of a punk house is a key factor in how long the house will last as a show space. When one considers the general chaos surrounding most shows, that time can be extended if the neighborhood is right. The stories that people tell about how their houses function relative to police and landlords are nuanced but share many themes.

Because the Coach House is located in Lincoln Park, one of Chicago's wealthier neighborhoods, the cops should have been quick to shut down the Coke Bust show. But they didn't, which runs counter to most policing strategies related to punk houses. At the same time, that was the last show booked in that space, so the police ignored the noise that night; I am guessing the landlord was less forgiving. Since most punks are looking for large houses with cheap rent and a space to practice/host shows, those houses tend to exist in neighborhoods with a lower socio-economic standing, warehouse districts, or university districts, not areas populated by middle-class/upper-class residents like Lincoln Park.

Hoople Mansion is located in an older section of Fort Myers that Nevin describes as "the kind of place where the cops aren't going to come unless they have to." He explains that the police were much more concerned with other parts of the neighborhood. "There was a house on the end of the street that was a pay-by-the-week halfway house, where the landlord was reputed to have collected rent with a hammer. For a couple years the cops were there almost every day. That didn't really impact us. We weren't buying or selling drugs and we weren't in the prostitution rings and all that shit, so we just kind of had our little thing there."

Nevin adds that the relationship they had with the landlord contributed to the lack of problems at Hoople Mansion. "She was tickled pink that we were living there," he says. "The last tenants did tons of damage and they had locks on the outside of the doors. They had Guatemalan laborers locked in." He notes that his crew did not inform the landlord right away that they would be doing shows, but after the first few went off without problems, they explained what they were doing. "We did some repairs for her and she would cut us a break on the rent. She kind of trusted us by the time we told her. That house just worked out: the police situation was right, landlord situation was right. I know those stars don't always align. We most certainly had a good deal going with all of that."

Mouth House had a similar astronomical alignment at first. Clay Dehaan tells me that the landlord prefers renting to larger groups of people. "It's a really big house and I think she would make more money if she broke it up into apartments, charged individually, and fixed up the house. She doesn't want to do that. Before us there was a bike co-op living there that was more on the hippie edge. They trashed the place as well, although they didn't have nearly as many shows. So she knows what to expect." She basically is willing to trade not being hassled by tenants while they are living there for having to repair the house when tenants move out, although video footage of Mouth House shows a truly dilapidated dump so she either wasn't messing with repairs or didn't know what she'd be dealing with when the Mouth House tenants moved out.

Having a low-key landlord—which can mean anything from fixing major problems but leaving the rest of the troubles to be solved by the tenants to the full on qualities of a slum lord—makes it easier to host shows. As Josh Otten explains to me about FSU Garage, he and Jeff Eaton from Modern Life is War looked at a variety of houses to rent, some of which were really nice (and perhaps too nice, since they were seeking a place where shows could happen). "But then there was this shitty little—it wasn't even a five bedroom—but the guy sold it to us as, 'You know you can fit five people in here and rent will be super cheap.' It was just this piece of shit. We checked the basement at first and the basement's a little small. And then he showed us this garage, and we're like, 'Holy shit. You know this would be perfect. All we need to do is figure out a way to soundproof it. You got a good amount of space here. This would be great.'" Josh explains that the landlord was "really hands-off the entire time." It seems that both parties set a tone when they met at the house. "We sort of started a thing right from the get-go that we were dirty kids and we don't really care either that this house is shitty. You know, we're not gonna have any problems or we'll try to fix it ourselves if something comes up. If you stay out of our business, we won't bother you at all. I think in the five or six years that we lived in that house we may have called him once or twice."

Josh and his friends soon found a way to soundproof the garage when there was a flood in one of the University of Northern Iowa dorms. "We were always dumpster diving at the dorms and stuff and they had thrown out a ridiculous amount of mattresses. We were like, 'Yeah, this will be great for soundproofing.' At the same time, all the kids are moving out of the dorms and they all have little square carpets and this will be perfect to sound proof it as well. We started going around collecting this carpet and these mattresses, and then we found out that in town there's a mattress factory." When people bought new mattresses the company would deliver those mattresses and take customers' old mattresses, which were then tossed in dumpsters at the factory. "So we'd go and check out all these mattresses. We'd give them the smell test to make sure they hadn't been peed on. This place also did carpet, so they'd have these huge rolls of carpet. And so we'd go and we just kept collecting these materials." Josh and his housemates nailed the carpet along the walls of the garage and lined the rafters and walls/garage door with the mattresses. "It's a residential neighborhood [laughs], so we don't want the noise to carry."

Adding mattresses and carpeting to the FSU Garage are temporary changes, but other tenants make more radical alterations to houses to create show space options. "We were fortunate enough to have landlords who didn't really care what we did so long as the rent got in on time," says Sean Murphy of Whitney House in Hartford, Connecticut in an interview with Paul J. Comeau in the April 2011 issue of *MRR*. Hosting shows at Whitney House wasn't as simple as cleaning up the basement and inviting bands to play. Murphy says that he and his roommates "had one of those Field of Dreams moments where we're like, we can tear down these walls and put up walls here, and just make a decent basement space." He adds that the landlord knows that they are doing shows in the house and doesn't care as long as the rent is paid on time.

Landlords understand that the age of the renters and the location of the house will influence how the tenants care for the house. "The neighborhood we're in is Five Points, which ten to twenty years ago had a really bad reputation for drugs and crime," Clay tells me. "It's really not so bad these days; it's getting gentrified a lot. There's condos going up all around. But the police presence is still really low. Across the street we have subsidized housing, we have an empty lot on one side, and across the street is an elementary school." Five Points has historically been a Black neighborhood, famous for jazz bars and discussed by Jack Kerouac in *On the Road*. Now, Clay says, African Americans and Latin American immigrants primarily populate the area (although census data shows that the largest group within the official boundaries are Whites).

Multi-ethnic, working-class neighborhoods often feature an approach to public life that runs counter to the stereotypically sedate middle-class housing districts. Al Pist emphasizes, "The neighbors weren't the kind of people to call the cops. The neighbors had a lot [of] loud parties and stuff. I don't think that they were going to call the cops if noise was a problem for them. They wouldn't want us to return the favor when they had a loud party at their house," Al tells me. "I would say that it was a lower-middle-class, racially-mixed neighborhood. We had a Puerto Rican family on one side of us. They had a lot of really loud parties. And the other guy next to us was an older white guy who was almost completely deaf. And the people across the street were riding pocket bikes all hours of the night up and down the street."

Ghost House had a similar socio-geographic advantage given the house's proximity to downtown Lincoln, Nebraska. Vic Vicars explains that the house was mostly surrounded by light industry that operated during business hours (a freight warehouse, an auto body shop) and they benefitted from the history of the house being rented to college students. There were very few houses around them and the housing that did exist in the neighborhood was rented to residents who were less likely to call the police. The landlord "was apathetic as long as we paid the rent on time. Or, if there was too much trash, he would send me a text and ask that we cleaned up the trash." Vic adds, "there was definitely illegal drug production happening in the house next door to us. Occasionally cops would come but there were other problems in this neighborhood."

Although Chicago is home to a lot of universities, the city lacks the features that one associates with college towns (most notably clearly defined university housing districts, including fraternity and sorority houses). Matt's reflection about Chicago PD being confused by types of loud noises is extremely applicable to many college towns in the U.S., where loud parties are part of the sonic realities for residents. Punks who host shows in such neighborhoods have far fewer problems with police and landlords, who like Josh's landlord, Clay's landlord, or Vic's landlord, understand that college-aged renters are a demographic that is concerned about parties and are likely less responsible when it comes to care for the residence.

James Payne explains to me that in Columbus the area around Ohio State University is known as Campus even though much of that locale is not part of the OSU campus. He says that there are a lot of punk houses in that general area "because in Columbus at the OSU Campus the cops just don't come to house shows." He references Legion of Doom, one of the longer-running houses in the country, and mentions "a house called 15th House that's been there for a decade. A house I had later called the Monster House had at least a show a week for four years and we only dealt with the cops twice I think." Columbus is the third largest metropolitan area in Ohio, but the quantity of students at OSU helps distinguish Columbus from other cities in the U.S. James thinks that the college town vibe contributes to the longevity of punk houses there. "No one's gonna complain about the noise; it's no better or no worse than any other party that's on Campus." Zack Furness references Columbus as a comparable geographic experience when reflecting on his time in State College, Pennsylvania: "The place at Penn State was two blocks from the main drag of one of the biggest areas of fraternities in the country other than maybe Ohio State, so we never had the cops called on us for shows there and never really got called on for practice either."

James notes, "I was at my first house and I remember the cops coming, and for whatever reason we didn't let them in," he explains to me. "Actually it was really stupid because they would have just let me off with a warning but I was really young and dumb and we didn't want to talk to them. I ended up getting a noise violation. But I ran shows in houses forever after that, like six years on Campus, and never have received another noise violation."

Iowa City is another college town with an active punk scene. Like Columbus and State College, the student housing areas are less regulated. Joe Milik explains that his current house is ideally located for shows. "On one side my friend lives there and is in a band, so he's not going to call the cops on us. On the other side was this really old lady and we assume she's deaf because she's never called the cops on us ever, and we have thrown some dumb, insane, stupid shows that go way too late. Behind us is a house where these 50-year-old Juggalo guys live. They don't give a shit about anything or they'll be like, 'Hey guys, it's 1:00 a.m. can you wrap this up?' if we're being too loud." Joe adds that they never have problems with police if the show ends before midnight. Difficulties tend to arise when shows run longer, but in those instances the police break up the show as they would any other college party. "Iowa City is a college town, so the cops aren't going to discern between a house party and a house show," Joe says. Residents are also used to loud house parties, but they will call the police if the noise is egregious and things get too crazy. "Yeah, there's a limit, but it seems that in Iowa City it's a bit higher than other places."

Doing shows in a college town can also produce some strange situations that other punks would not encounter, since house shows in non-college towns tend to attract punks who are part of the scene or friends of people who are into punk. Joe notes that most shows draw that same type of crowd, which is usually about 30 people. "We've had 100 people there once, and that was a situation where I was surprised that the cops didn't get called because it was a show thrown right at the beginning of the semester so kids are back in town wanting to party. There's kids wandering the streets looking for parties and they'd come by our house and hear this loud music. All these girls in bras and panties and body paint showed up. It was weird." He says that the people who wanted to see the bands were able to fit into the basement but the rest just hung out in the house. "There were like 50 people down there. Everyone else was there because they wanted to witness a spectacle that they just so happened to come across while walking around Iowa City, I guess."

Lost Cross is located in an area mostly filled with Southern Illinois University student renters. The person who owns the house also owns the house next door. Patrick Houdek tells me that he can't remember the police showing up during a show. However, he recalls a night when the fire department showed up. One of the locals somehow came into "one of those military grade smoke bombs. It's not often that you get a chance to light one of those things off, so you don't really know what's gonna... And he lit it off in the basement during No Empathy's set and it was kind of near the furnace so a friend of ours who lived next door thought the house was on fire." By the time the fire department arrived most people were out of the house, although the band kept playing AC/DC's "T.N.T." "The fire department tried to give him [the primary tenant] a ticket for having too many people in the basement, but he said, 'There's people in the backyard, there's people in the living room, there's not too many people.' He didn't get a ticket."

Mike Seamans from Mind Cure Records explains that the university district in Pittsburgh was also wild, but there were multiple layers of policing. "Depending on where you are, you might get university police, not Pittsburgh police officers." Shows did get shut down, he tells me, which was understandable. "You'd have these crazy shows with sixteen- or seventeen-year-old kids with mohawks puking in the street. They weren't inconspicuous by any means."

One of the major differences between punk houses in college towns and houses in working-class neighborhoods is the ways that a neighborhood can change. University districts tend to change when the universities buy up land and expand their influence in a city. This will sometimes affect housing used for punk shows. As Mike says about Pittsburgh, "All this space was up for grabs and when there is nobody to bother, no one really cares if there are a bunch of people with mohawks on the front lawn drinking 40s who happen to be seventeen years old. Who is gonna care? And suddenly it's a place they're trying to make look appealing to get more students." The presence of a university can contribute to the gentrification of an area, but student housing districts are rarely attractive neighborhoods for home buyers who tend to be linked with gentrification. The housing stock is usually rundown and the neighborhoods are too wild. Working-class neighborhoods, though, can change in ways that have a broader influence on how underground culture can be created and fostered. Clay's comment that Five Points is gentrifying speaks to this point.

Gentrification refers to the class remake of an urban neighborhood. With the influx of wealthier (and often whiter) residents come expectations that the police will be present, which should deter crime but also control behaviors deemed to interfere with a middle-class quality of life. The police then start to pay more attention to the houses that stand out from others, which is, in part, what happened to Mouth House shortly after I interviewed Clay.

Two members of Denver hardcore band Negative Degree told me before one of their shows in Chicago that Mouth House was busted during a very chaotic sting executed by undercover and uniformed cops. Bree Davies describes the closing of Mouth House in greater detail in *Westword*, Denver's alternative weekly. Apparently vice cops led the effort to shut down the Halloween show. One tenant, who was quoted anonymously, explained to Bree that the cops were looking for drugs or alcohol. Citations were issued to two of the residents and the landlord followed with an eviction notice. As with the police efforts in Boston,

Denver PD's bust was informed by intelligence gathered from the Internet. Bree quotes the same anonymous tenant, who identifies Songkick as the major problem. Songkick is a website that lists concerts throughout the U.S. Unlike MySpace, Twitter, or Facebook, users do not create private event listings or make announcements about shows. The inclusion of Mouth House shows created the appearance that the house was a venue selling tickets even though the common DIY practice of collecting donations was used there. It's interesting (in a problematic way) that a mainstream tool that has nothing to do with the underground drew some attention to the underground. Allowing mainstream industries into the underground is never going to benefit punks in the long run (and rarely in the short term).

If an informational website influenced the police in Denver in ways that mirrored Boston PD information gathering through social media websites, that is where the similarities between the two police actions end. "The cops said that they weren't here to bust the show; they were here for the alcohol," the tenant tells Bree. "But we weren't running a speakeasy—it was a donation thing, and there happened to be a keg. We never intended it to be like, '$5, here's your alcohol.' That was just a side aspect of it—we were doing what we always do—having a DIY show." I had talked with Patrick Houdek well before Mouth House shut down and he was adamant that one reason Lost Cross has been able to avoid police pressure for so long, even though the Lost Cross has a party house feel, is directly connected the lack of kegs at their shows. A keg makes sense financially in a BYOB party house, but the appearance of selling alcohol (including selling alcohol to minors) is a recipe for problems with the police, as the punks at Mouth House discovered.

There is not an explicit link between the gentrification of Five Points and the actions of the Denver PD, since the police were focused on the mistaken belief that Mouth House was charging admission and that entrance fee included access to the keg. At the same time, to disregard links between gentrification and policing Five Points would be a mistake. Given the actions of gentrifiers in other gentrifying cities throughout the U.S., a loud show space will run counter to the desired aesthetics of those people, who will in turn raise concerns with the police.

James Payne now lives at Skylab Gallery in Columbus. His experiences in this downtown space are very different from the university district where he lived and booked shows in the past, and exemplify how people who gentrify an area will expect a specific soundscape and lifetyle in their new neighborhood. He explains to me that a lot less people live downtown compared to other parts of Columbus. "Almost everyone that lives down there that isn't living in my building specifically are young professionals and they do call the cops on us. The current space that I'm living in has been there since 1999 and it's not strictly a punk house; there's an art gallery and it's more experimental noise. And there are meetings and art openings, movies. But when there are shows, they're usually really loud. And there are a lot of dance nights or whatever. Lately the cops have been coming and it's really annoying."

Richard Lloyd wrote in his book, *Neo-Bohemia*, that there is an important irony in the tensions between middle-class desires and actual urban experiences. New residents to bohemian sections of a city are seeking hip encounters in so-called authentic neighborhoods but their arrival destroys the very experience they crave. And when we break down how they live, really they are seeking a gritty aesthetic that can be twinned with middle-class accouterments, or the energy of a particular district without the hassles of real urban encounters. They want art galleries, independent cafes, and record stores (so they can frame the sleeves on their exposed brick walls), but as James notes, they don't actually want the noise that comes with shows in a gallery space. This wave of gentrifiers moves to an area for the vibe, but that they eventually change the vibe through their own actions and presence.

I published an article in 2010 titled "Bring on the Shock Troops" that critically examined how the press represents artist-led gentrification. Punk houses would certainly fit the general schema in that young (primarily White and often middle-class) bohemians move into an area because the rent is cheap and the spaces are large enough to engage in a variety of art-related projects. Moreover, the demographics and feel of such neighborhoods are the polar opposite of the suburbs, which are usually represented as oppressive in experience and design. The press likes to refer to these arty-types as "urban pioneers" when these people first move into the neighborhoods and then the same bohmians are referred to as victims of gentrification when the yuppies arrive. I problematized that narrative in a number of ways, primarily focusing on the artists as the first gentrifiers. They might not possess the economic wealth normally linked with the gentry, but they infuse a cultural capital into the area and are often seen as desirable by landlords and developers. The class remake begins because class encompasses more than just socioeconomic status; class also includes education and occupation. Bringing this back to punk spaces, some punks are formally educated and work in creative industries while others are self-educated. And punk spaces can add a creative edge to an area.

Punks might not like to think of themselves as a group that has facilitated the gentrification of an area, but this is exactly what they do when they host shows, open cafes and record stores, start pizza by the slice places, and found bike co-ops in neighborhoods that previously lacked a punk presence. Therefore, the socio-geographic features that influence where punks decide to book shows means that some areas will change because punks have contributed to the cultural cachet of those neighborhoods, especially in warehouse districts, downtown areas, and multi-ethnic neighborhoods close to mass transportation.

I think there are ways that punks can integrate into a neighborhood without imitating the shift toward a hipster haven, but such situations need to happen in places where there is already some broader sense of what punk can mean relative to a more demographically diverse scene. Zack Furness lived in Chicago prior to moving back to Pittsburgh and reflects on the various scenes here that model some level of integration into a neighborhood. "I was used to playing for almost entirely white kids, but between Rancho Huevos and some of the shows we played on the West Side of town, it was much more interesting than some of the things I would go to on the North Side, even if it was touring bands." He specifically mentions the ways that these shows on the South and West Sides of the city often attracted a more diverse collection of punks. "I would meet punks from Peru, El Salvador, and lots of Mexican punks. These were people who were connected to punk being a counterculture and not just music." There have been some gentrification pressures within some Chicago neighborhoods that have historically been populated by Mexican immigrants and Mexican Americans. These areas are attractive because rent is cheaper and the spaces are often larger. The art scenes in these neighborhoods are another attraction for various countercultural types (including punks), who want to live where there are creative activities and perhaps cultural allies.

Some punks move into more traditionally defined family-oriented neighborhoods that might be categorized as working class or lower-middle class. These areas are also risky because shifts in housing prices can lead middle-class families guided by a middle-class ethos to look to such areas when priced out of more traditional middle-class residential districts. For example, George Myers explains to me that after leaving the Schoolhouse, he and two other roommates moved into a home in a residential neighborhood in Western Massachusetts, where they continued to book shows. The house is well-located, since there is "an incredible amount of white noise" in the area, generated in part by a pot-hole laden freight road and also a nearby community music center. "We had really monstrously loud stuff. And we never had trouble. But I'm playing rinky-dink 4/4 drum beats and the cops show up? I couldn't even connect that they would be there for me; it made no sense. Then he said, 'We had a noise complaint.' What the hell? So it must be this family [a new couple with a young child that recently moved into a house across the street]. I don't begrudge them; they must have a reason for it. I try to be empathetic, but it's like, 'Man, we've been here for a very long time doing this and nobody's had a problem with it.' The whole neighborhood didn't speak up for that long and then one family...," George says, trailing off.

Jenny Ray describes a similar scenario that led to the end of the Bike House, which had been a recurring site of concern for neighbors. "Our house was one house off a pretty busy street. It was almost like a drag, if you will, called Lower Greenville," Jenny

Ray tells me. "It's always funny because our house was just this eyesore in between and amidst these McMansions because they were gentrifying the area. We're just this grimy, gross punk house in the middle of all these nice houses, but we didn't care so we just kept doing it." Eventually, the neighbors had had enough and started calling the police. The cops appeared regularly, issuing Jenny and her housemates a ticket based on the noise complaint. "The officer was like, 'The next time I come back someone's going to jail.' So I was like, 'Dudes we can't have shows anymore. I'm not going to jail.'"

Many of the people I interviewed explained that neighbors (usually new residents in the neighborhood) should just talk with the punks about concerns. This makes sense; it is the neighborly thing to do, which I know sounds circular. Of course, the punks could be less passive and initiate the conversations. Furthermore, one has to wonder if the new residents are merely replicating the same lack of neighborly qualities that the punks enacted when moving into these area. At one point the punks were the new residents, but most punks don't reach out to the residents that were living in the same neighborhoods when the punks arrived.

I ask Jenny if she tried to talk with her neighbors about the shows at the Bike House, perhaps to find some middle ground where they could host shows but find a better ending time that could make the neighbors happy. She says that she and her housemates hadn't made that effort. "They would come over and yell at us basically and insult us. There wasn't a point to it. When you have a house show you try to get it over by midnight. The partying didn't stop, so I know they did not care for us at all. I don't think it would have made a difference even if we had tried to build some sort of relationship with them. I know that seems kind of insolent, but rich people we didn't care about or know when we just wanted punk shows. You're gonna complain either way, so..."

Realistically, Jenny was in a no-win situation in terms of trying to continue doing shows. Given my experiences with a house located behind my apartment building where there was a range of problems (including tenants in my building finding a bag filled with bullets in our shared backyard with that

house), I assume that Jenny's neighbors likely considered the house itself—as a physical structure—to be at least 50 percent of the problem: a run-down dwelling that reflects a slumlord's lack of concern for the neighborhood. Punk shows at the Bike House probably functioned as a problematic sonic add-on for the neighbors. In fact, Jenny explains to me that they were the last tenants in the house, which was leveled after she and her housemates moved out.

Clay tells me that some of his neighbors have been bothered by the shows at Mouth House. "They have told me personally, 'Oh, your music kept me up.'" But such responses didn't change Mouth House's late night hours. "Our shows start here around 10:30 and that's normal for every DIY space in town. Everyone expects a DIY show here to start late and go late. We try to cut it off at about 1:00 a.m." They kept going with these times because they were confident that the neighbors "would never call the cops because they're not that type of people." Clay's description of dealing with neighbors is not unique. Punks are in a difficult position given punk's history and politics. Bending show times to meet the demands of a neighborhood wouldn't be well-received in punk circles. Similarly, trying to start and end shows earlier might hurt the bands, since punks are going to show up when punks show up. But just because DIY spaces have historically started and ended shows at specific times doesn't mean the next house needs to follow these patterns. Different neighborhoods might require varied approaches. Moreover, saying that something is done in a certain way "because that's how punks have done it in the past" is a strange type of conformity that doesn't feel very punk either.

Mickie Rat tells me, though, that there are lessons that punks can learn about managing time and negotiating space in their neighborhoods in an effort to extend the life of the house. "There were some fuckups, learning how late to take a show before people would start complaining or people would call the cops," he says about Casa de Chaos. "You also learn that if you let a bunch of people hang out on the sidewalk in front of your house drinking beer, it would attract more attention. After a while we learned to keep everybody in the backyard and go, 'Hey, don't bring the cops out here by drinking 40s in front of the house. Stay in the backyard so they don't know we're here.'" Because Casa is in the Barmuda Triangle, with its eight bars in a six-block radius, the culture of the area is different than the other neighborhoods. "There are always people walking up and down the streets, yelling, fighting, screaming at each other, getting way too drunk, drunk driving and crashing into parked cars," Mickie explains. "It's a wild part of town, so that helped with keeping the cops away because they're usually at one of the eight bars around the house. It's almost a little bit bulletproof in that way. Stuff can probably get a little bit out of control and they probably won't notice, but I never took that for granted. I always tried to cover my ass in whatever way that I could."

Casa is one of the longest running punk houses in the U.S., so it has been able to avoid the types of neighborhood changes that have occurred in other areas around the country where younger couples move in to be close to nightlife but want a more tempered scene once they've got property investments to consider and a family to raise. In theory, the Barmuda Triangle could change in ways that mirror other gentrified neighborhoods; however, such a full-scale transformation seems unlikely. It's one thing to move into a working-class neighborhood and help usher in changes given the lack of political power that renters have, but it's another thing to try to force changes among business owners. The history of frat houses and bars in the area means Casa de Chaos is in a rare sweet spot where negotiating with the neighbors is less of a factor. Again, Mickie figured out early on that the best approach is to identify the intersection of how late a show can run and how to keep out of sight to avoid upsetting neighbors and garnering the attention of the cops.

As might be expected, there seems to be a lot fewer hassles with neighbors and police when punks are doing shows at their parents' houses. It helps if those houses are not in heavily populated areas, since shows in a more stereotypically middle-class suburb can still face some pressures from the police even if the family is integrated into the community. For example, Jim Gies tells me that he did a few shows at his mom's suburban house when he was in high school. "Putting the touring band in the middle I figured out early because the cops showed up at my mom's house a couple times," says Jim. "I don't want it to be a situation where the band from out of town can't play."

Reflecting on the longevity of The Shed, John Boilard believes a combination of geography and demographics helped. There were only four or five houses on the street "that would be close enough to even know that something was happening. One of the neighbors was never ever home/traveled a lot and the others had parties themselves, so it worked out that they could be loud and we could be loud but it ended by 10:00 or 11:00." John and Mike Swiatlowski knew that the noise ordinance violations began at 11:00 p.m. so they ended shows before then. Also, The Shed was a sober space, so they were also protected against the other main issue that could lead to the police shutting down a show: underage drinking. John tells me that even though he was a teenager, his mom expected that he and his friends would deal with the police if they came to the house. "She would usually say, 'If the cops come, it's up to you. This is your show, so you deal with it. But if you need me, come get me.' I feel like we became experts at dealing with the cops. 'Oh, the band's from Hawaii and they came all the way here to play. We just need twenty more minutes.'"

John notes, though, that the neighborhood changed when construction started on a new housing development, which brought new people to the area and created a more densely packed street. Knowing that the neighborhood dynamics were shifting, John, Mike, and their friends took an approach from which many punks could learn. "At this point, we would do a show at the end of the year that was almost like a benefit for the neighbors. We would raise a little money to buy them passes for the movies, bake them cookies, do whatever we could do to say thank you. Go to their house and say, 'Thanks for putting up with our noise; we appreciate it. We mostly take the winter off. If there are ever any problems, please let us know. Here's our number, call us.'"

These efforts seemed to appease most of the neighbors, or if nothing else, help the neighbors get to know John and his friends rather than viewing them as strange kids down the street who make a lot of noise. However, as Jenny experienced with her neighbors, some residents won't be able to look beyond the aggressive style of music and see a person who is trying to do something creative. These types of neighbors expect a very private, and generally quiet, standard of living. This was the case with one of John's neighbors. "We would get the cops coming, funnily enough, when we weren't even there," John tells me. "There were several shows that we would do at other locations and we would meet at The Shed and then carpool four of five miles into the woods and the neighbors would see cars there and think, 'Oh, there's a show.' They would call the cops. The cops would show up and my mom was there by herself. 'There's been no one here for hours.' At that point we knew this was a little bit of bullshit. We narrowed it down to one neighbor, who, when it came to the end of the year, wouldn't open the door for us. They were like, 'Yeah, yeah, leave it on the porch.' The funny thing is that the year we stopped doing it, that couple broke up and the woman who had the problem with the shows moved. I moved, we stopped the shows for a number of reasons, but part of it was because of the neighbors."

John is not the only person who tells me about trying to coordinate with neighbors but his crew was proactive about meeting people in the neighborhood and clarifying what was happening with the shows, which is rare. For example, Josh explains that the FSU Garage residents had not been in contact with neighbors for the first year or two that they were doing shows. "I want to say that it went about two years before our first run in with the cops. I think a neighbor complained because they said somebody spray-painted something on the ground in front of their house and somebody's car was keyed. Something like that." Josh repeats a point that he stressed when he told me about the shows at the Coliseum in Marshalltown, Iowa: they were always good about trying to police themselves. Josh and his friends understood that they would be shut down if the punks brought negative attention to the scene. Between sets, kids who came to shows at FSU Garage were encouraged to stay in the house, the garage, or the area between these two buildings rather than hanging out in front or wandering around the neighborhood. "When that first cop came, he didn't believe us that there were bands playing. And we were like, 'Thank God, you know, that's good.' We were trying to be super-respectful, super-nice." The police officer did not break up the show or write a noise violation; he seemed to be more focused on the kids that were hanging between the house and the garage and the noise that was being generated from a group of punks talking loudly. Josh and the other residents were told to keep people in the garage.

"That next day we set up a campaign to go talk to the neighbors. Basically to apologize for anything that anyone might have done. And to say that if damage was done, to let us know so we could take care of it and we were trying our best to keep that from happening. We told them what was going on. We said that we have friends in bands all across the country looking for places to play, and by that point all the neighbors pretty much knew what we did because they'd see a band with equipment or one of those short buses parked outside. 'We've known you've been doing that' blahblahblah. And so we straightened it out with the neighbors fairly well, and we went on a while longer with it."

Cam Myers adds that FSU Garage ended when the police started coming more regularly. Punks in the house were caught in a vicious circle. "Word got out that there was a bunch of mattresses in there and we had to take those to the dump, but then there was no soundproofing so it was really loud." He echoes Josh's claim that the police were surprisingly cool about the situation, basically stating that the either bands need to be quieter or the show has to stop. "The second-to-last show we did the police came right when the first band started. They were like, 'No, it's not happening tonight. You gotta stop.' The entire show moved across town to a different house and they did the show in the basement of that house. I don't think that house went on to do more shows so it was more like come on over and have a party." The last show at FSU Garage actually happened in the basement since they knew the garage was not going to work. As with the Bike House, when the punks moved out of FSU Garage, the house was sold and demolished. The site is now part of a strip mall.

It is obviously rare that punks will live in area where there is a broader acceptance of (or appreciation for) a barrage of noise. Given this experiential reality, I think it's really important that punks consider how their actions affect their neighbors and strive to work within a neighborhood to integrate smoothly into that area. Making such efforts can prolong the life of a house and developing these relationships might also extend the reach of punk within that neighborhood. Liz Pelly writes in her *Boston Phoenix* article about the noise ordinance that she is "not suggesting that music lovers should be allowed to disrupt their neighbors and destroy their quality of life. But this new noise ordinance would encourage folks to call the police every time they hear a noisy guitar riff or the pound of a drum—rather than walk over to their neighbor's house and fostering a community dialogue, working together to meet everyone's needs." This is an important point. DIY punk shows are often explicitly connected to a belief in community, but such community efforts don't exist in isolation. The ideals that guide connections among punks, should inform other relationships, including how punks interact with their neighbors.

There is a common phrase used among punks that borrows a Germs song/EP title: What We Do is Secret. Given the contributions of social media to DIY space closures in Boston and Denver, it's understandable why punks believe that being secretive can buffer against problems. At the same time, I have always been drawn to punk as a way of being in the world. I think that way of being is not exclusive to current punks, but instead is a model for everyone. I understand that many people won't like the music, but I think they can make sense of what it means to do things themselves, to make culture rather than strictly consume culture, and to consider opportunities for community engagement rather than individual isolation. Connecting with one's neighbors can humanize people in the punk house and put some faces with the racket that neighbors hear, which might inspire a degree of patience rather than a quick call to the police. And such efforts might help kids in the area, who are not currently part of the scene, consider how they might find a home in punk. As Zack Furness says to me on neighborhood politics: "If I have a gripe about the way that punks do shows, it's that I don't like it when people do shows where they are not inviting to people who live in the neighborhood." Although houses in bigger scenes can segregate sounds rather than mixing bills, this does not extend to smaller scenes, where punks work with what they can. The variety of styles presented on a mixed bill might feature something that can appeal to the very people Zack identifies as being excluded from the shows.

Some punks will not be able to engage neighbors for a variety of complicated reasons, as Jenny explained about the Bike House and John discussed with the family that would not open the door when he and his friends offered an end-of-the-year gift. There are other situations where the neighborhood can work for house shows given the general social life of the area, but trying to find some connection with the neighbors is not going to be possible. For example, Karin and Lance observe in a June 1990 *MRR* interview with Filth that "there seems to be a whole scene with parties." A party in this instance refers to alternatives to 924 Gilman and clubs in the Bay Area. Members of Filth have been involved with this relatively new alternative, although the recent closing of Jim's basement disappoints them. "There's gunfire in our neighborhood every night. But this night a dog got shot. So we went out to see if it was our dog that got shot and it wasn't," Jim explains. "So the cops came by about ten minutes later. There was about twenty guys in this house who went running back in except for the lookout guy. He just brushed off the cops and got rid of them." The other guys returned to the front yard after the police left. The lookout guy then "pointed at our window saying that we had called the cops on them. Which is what we avoid doing. So they came across the street and surround the house. We had to get the police to escort us out." Jake adds that the "neighborhood is fucked. But the house is great for parties." Lenny, reflecting the spirit of so many punks who came before and after, says: "I think it put like seven people out of their living spaces. So give it a little more time and there will be another one." This was clearly a living situation where working with the neighbors was not going to be an option, but in radically different ways than other punks have experienced. Punks might have felt chased out by middle-class neighbors, but the threat of physical violence is not a standard reason for houses closing in recent times.

Although the physical threats against punks have subsided in the past two decades, the obstacles to creating and sustaining houses for DIY shows remain. For example, punks continue devising tactics to evade the police. Bull Gervasi describes a Policy of 3 show in Santa Cruz, California with Bleed and Spitboy at a gallery space. "Before the show even started the cops showed up so it was shut down. Then there was the scramble to move it to somebody's house," says Bull. "It was such a great show. It was really packed. It was really hot. There was a sense of excitement because the other one was shut down and we weren't sure if the cops were going to show up and shut this one down. We were trying to rush through, so everyone was sharing equipment and playing short sets. But it was just really great, a really fun show."

When Bob Suren described to me the creative spaces punks sought out in South Florida in an effort to evade the police, the tone of his stories conjured the thrill of the chase and an awareness of what it means to be able to do a punk show in the face of various official obstacles. But this buzz is short-lived when police bust a show, landlords threaten eviction, or neighbors cause problems. These aggravations often lead to burnout. And sometimes punks shift their focus and seek out other DIY alternatives that, on the surface, will be more stable.

Making a Scene

"You know, sometimes these things happen," says a white guy with a scraggly beard and a black eye. He shrugs his shoulders and makes a "such is life" facial expression that complements his matter-of-fact phrasing. The black eye is a product of getting elbowed while dancing at a show last week. He laughs and then tells me about going to work with a variety of punk rock wounds. "At first the other people in the kitchen where I work were worried, thinking that I was getting into fights, but over time they expected me to arrive with various scrapes and bruises." An elbow to the eye, a foot in the chest, a knee in the back, a sweaty arm across the face are all forms of physical contact that can be expected when people dance at punk shows, especially hardcore shows. Usually anything more extreme is accidental and often followed by an apology from the offender.

The flyer for this Dropdead, Ruidosa Inmundicia, and Sick Fix show at Democracy Center in Boston is explicit about putting the Punx back in punctual; however, this 5:00 p.m. show is running on egregious punk time, not the usual one-hour-behind schedule punk time. Those who arrived on normal punk time are hanging around outside. Some people chitchat with friends; others mess around with their phones in an effort to look like they have something to do; a few soak in the warm September sun and people watch; and others talk with strangers, as I am doing with the scraggly beard guy. Nobody seems on edge. This relaxed energy, like the current state of communal dancing, is radically different from what many punks experienced twenty years ago. As Jade Tree records co-owner Darren Walters wrote in his contribution to the edited collection, *My First Time*, describing a Circle Jerks, Agnostic Front, and Last Stand show at City Gardens in Trenton, "The violence was plentiful, seemingly endless, and strangely carefree." He claims that during Agnostic Front's set, "the skins went nutso. All set long they took the dance floor as their battlefield and dared the unshaven to enter the pit." When the Circle Jerks played "more fights broke out as City Gardens' floor soaked up the blood. The show never ceased to be violent, it only ebbed and flowed."

Even subsets within punk that should have been grounded in a desire to build community through invitational actions and discourses had become violent. For example, some punks who identified as straight edge were so militant about their politics that they, like the skinheads, seemed to be embody a gang mentality. The youth crew influence was disappointing because there were many punks who shared the straight edge ideals. They believed in not drinking or doing drugs so a clear mind engaged in critical thinking could be prioritized, chose not to eat meat, and believed that political coalitions could be grounded in these beliefs. As Kent McLard wrote in the liner notes to the Ebullition compilation, *XXX: Some Ideas are Poisonous*, there were many punks who identified as straight edge, but had no interest in signing up for the brocore vision of punk that had become the more common representation of the straight edge philosophy. And yet straight edge had become firmly associated with clean-cut white kids wearing sports jerseys and the latest kicks, kids who transferred a stereotypically jock mentality from the basketball court to the punk show.

"In the earlier part of the '90s we were still going to some of those shows with the New York hardcore bands but we made a conscious decision not to be part of that. Us as a band [Policy of 3], the Cabbage Collective as a group in Philly, we didn't want anything to do with that macho dudefest violence," Bull Gervasi tells me. "We were trying to be the opposite of that; we wanted to be an inclusive space. Riot Grrrl and the emo scene were coming together. When we started the Cabbage Collective we wrote this manifesto about being an inclusive space. Some of those Jersey hardcore bands played our shows, but we never got into the macho kickboxing bands."

This scenario outside the Democracy Center provides a context to consider how DIY punk shows emerged out of this violent past through the actions of punks who wanted something different. The guy with the black eye and scraggly beard embodies a type of violence that has always been a feature of the punk show because the dancing usually involves aggressive forms of contact, but he also reflects how that violence is often enacted in punk in different ways now compared with the past. The occasional black eye from an elbow while dancing is not the same as attending fight night where a punk show seems to break out. Democracy Center and other volunteer-run DIY spaces have explicitly modeled a non-violent way of being together, through the communication of rules (often expressed in some play on the "No drugs, no alcohol, no jerks" slogan) and through the embodied communal actions of punks who volunteer at the space and who attend the shows. Thus, not only did the DIY touring network of the early 1990s usher in an alternative to mainstream touring practices, but DIY show spaces also provided more communal alternatives to the violent spaces that had become normalized in many punk scenes. Violence at DIY shows is now minimal because there are recurring conversations throughout the U.S. about sharing space at shows and because the cultural politics that informed DIY efforts in the 1990s have continued to become a more central feature of doing DIY punk today.

For people who are invested in the radical possibilities associated with punk, DIY spaces become key sites, allowing a different way of being together. As James Payne describes to me, "I was really invested in the notion of—Hakim Bey wrote about at the time, but I didn't know it then—temporary autonomous zones. The idea is that you could have a private space where you could create a sort of utopic atmosphere. Or whatever you didn't like about a macro political environment, you could create in a micro one." The key to this microenvironment was meeting like-minded punks and working together to make a scene.

Jake from Parasol MA and Peeple Watchin' describes a similar inspiration, about a decade after James', highlighting how much punk has progressed during that decade. "It was really political for me because here is a way for an entire community, that was globalized in a sense, to function outside the basic assumptions of capitalist profit motive, outside the basic assumptions of what is needed to make things work." He was most inspired by the ways that people without formal training or specialized skills, and who lacked access to capital, could make an alternative to mainstream music production. "The point for me about playing music is to play to enough people that I can talk to after the show." Jake adds that he quickly discovered that the political ideals that motivated his involvement in punk, also needed to animate challenges within the scene. "You really have to do things that seem uncomfortable and counterintuitive, such as 'policing the space,' and making sure that boundaries are maintained and are agreed upon by everybody. At least everybody that it's important to be involved there, getting this baseline like, 'This is our space so we can set some boundaries and we want to make it inclusive to the people who the rest of the fucking world isn't fucking inclusive to. You know, that's our priority.'"

Even as the punk house is opened up, transforming a private living space to a pseudo-public show space, the house still remains private. People section off parts of their houses that are not open to punks who attend shows. Similarly, in most cases, once the renters who are doing shows move out, the show space dies. Volunteer-run community spaces embody a different approach to the cultural politics of DIY punk because a single person does not own (or rent) the community space. The space is collectively run and, in theory, more stable in form, providing a connection between different generations of punks. Moreover, volunteer-run spaces often have implicit or explicit statements about the politics that guide the spaces—far more often than house spaces.

DIY volunteer-run spaces are created for a variety of reasons. Some punks have done house shows but need to stop because they are overwhelmed by having their houses become a semi-public space, nervous because of hassles with the cops, concerned about being evicted by landlords, and/or worn down by struggles with neighbors. The volunteer-run space starts to look like a better alternative. Other volunteer-run spaces are started because there are not house show options in a town or there aren't people who want to deal with the chaos of hosting shows in their houses. And some show spaces develop out of previously existing radical community spaces that have not done shows up to that point but are open to working with other like-minded groups. For example, Democracy Center was started as a space for community groups to hold meetings, but punks started booking shows there on weekends when the noise ordinance hours run later into the night.

Punks sought inspiration from community centers, parks, veterans halls, etc. Although these spaces can open up and then quickly close off to punk shows, such spaces were reference points for some of the first volunteer-run punk spaces because of multiple rooms that can be used for different types of creative activity and were open to various groups who are trying to foster some level of public engagement. Punks also understood the value of a space with a public presence, a key feature of many current volunteer-run spaces. If house spaces tend to rely on a level of secrecy, the volunteer-run space is grounded in a public declaration that a space run by and for punks can model alternative approaches to being together to enact a cultural politics. As Kimya Dawson writes in the book, *In Every Town*, she likes to play at volunteer-spaces because she knows that volunteers "want to be there—that it's not just a job for them."

David Ensminger experienced this level of energized participation in Rockford, Illinois in the late-1980s at a space called Rotation Station. "Originally it was a roller skating rink, but the guy Rory, whose mom ran it, converted it into a skateboard facility on the weekends." Rory's next move was to book shows at Rotation Station, beginning with some locals and then expanding to regional and national touring bands, such as Flag of Democracy. "Maybe fifteen of us knew them and everybody else was just skateboarding. We'd have pizza and by 10:00 or 11:00 it was time to go home. We did that for two years and that's how I learned about this tight knit, what we'd call high context, folk community where you learn the rituals."

"You could hang with the band. Sometimes those bands would literally end up back at my house," David remembers. He adds that Rotation Station was so important because it featured other punk resources in addition to the shows. "They had a little facility where you could buy trucks and wheels but you could also buy *Flipside* videos and skateboarding magazines. And I think you could buy fanzines there." There were opportunities to meet bands, to realize that the band members—many of whom were teenagers—have traveled across the country to play the same roller rink that one's friends were playing. "And then you would go and get your media and sometimes create your media for the next show: go make your flyer, use their Xerox machine there. And it was this whole world."

Rotation Station was a privately owned space. However, the experiences that David discusses in terms of having some control over what is booked, engaging with bands, and the space serving as an outlet for cultural life beyond the shows reflect the ideals that drove the creation of many of the early volunteer-run spaces. These same features inform contemporary efforts to develop new places. Similar to the experiences I described about Josh Otten and his friends booking The Coliseum in Marshalltown and Nevin Marshall and his friends booking the skate park in Fort Myers, David and his friends felt a sense of "we" even if there might have been one person who was taking charge or had access to the space. That collective "we" expands in a volunteer-run space context and is a key experiential feature for punks who contribute to running these DIY spaces.

Bull Gervasi tells me that this desire to work cooperatively with other punks inspired the formation of the Cabbage Collective in Philadelphia. "We basically posted a flyer at a bunch of the record stores in town. We're like, 'Hey, we want to start doing shows. We want it to be a collective effort. We're looking to do them in a DIY space so shows are affordable, bands get paid, people will feel safe, and we'll have tables where people can sell things and we'd have vegetarian food.'" Bull notes that members of the collective were inspired by the kind of internal and external forms of punk rock activism that were happening in the early 1990s. Their first meeting was a picnic. "A handful of folks showed up and were excited" about doing DIY shows, which started in 1993 at the Calvary Church. The shows were successful from various standpoints, claims Bull. "Basically potlucks at all the shows and people would sell T-shirts and patches and zines." He adds that the Cabbage Collective quickly established a reputation for doing good shows, hooking into a network of like-minded punks who were attempting to enact similar community-focused DIY punk show options in their cities. He specifically mentions ABC No Rio as a model and a cultural ally.

ABC No Rio is a true success story when considering long-lasting volunteer-run spaces, reflecting how a non-profit space can survive amidst a variety of economic and external political pressures. Matinee shows began there in December 1989, developing as an alternative to the violence-plagued norms at other spots (especially the matinee shows at CBGBs). In an April 2000 *MRR* interview with Arwen, Chris Boarts, who created the *Slug & Lettuce* zine, describes the energy that guided the development of ABC No Rio. "I was pretty much there as a die-hard regular volunteer. I missed the first show, but from the second show I was there, making fliers and doing whatever I could. That was my life, and it was great. You live and breathe it—it's intense," she notes. Chris adds that these everyday features of doing DIY punk existed alongside some larger struggles with the city. "ABC was a crack in the system, but it was a legit artist's community center, it wasn't a squat," she notes in reference to other efforts among punks in the Lower East Side of NYC to squat vacant buildings. Punks involved with those spaces were also part of the scene that was forming at ABC No Rio. Steven Englander explains to Kevin Erickson in *In Every Town* that they were paying rent to the city, but at various times people were living in the space (which may or may not have been legal).

Although the space was legal, there were periods when ABC No Rio experienced problems with its landlord: the city of New York. Sometimes rent was withheld so funds could be used to repair problems in the building and at other times the city was not cashing checks. During this time the city tried to move ABC No Rio to other city-owned spaces in Brooklyn, but people involved with No Rio fought to stay put at 156 Rivington, which felt like home. In 1997, after various protests and direct actions by ABC No Rio members and supporters, the city agreed to a conditional sale of the building for $1 with a variety of stipulations. That sale was finalized June 2006.

In a May 2006 *MRR* article about ABC No Rio by Vikki Law, Steven Englander explains that a range of questions continued to be asked by ABC No Rio volunteers during the time when there were concerns about losing the space: "What do you do if you don't have the space? How do you do No Rio programming without the space? One of the ideas was publication." Vikki adds that various alternatives to a physical space would be flawed, since "it's very difficult to publish a hardcore show or an improvised duet or the sense of camaraderie." To echo a phrase that I have used earlier in this book: space matters. ABC No Rio not only provides a site for punk shows (and other creative projects), but it is also the location from which interactions can occur among punks. The space is both a container for community and also a kind of matchmaking locale where punks form friendships, meet new acquaintances, and/or develop working relationships. This point is reflected in Vikki's article when she mentions gatherings at a neighborhood rice and beans spot after an ABC No Rio event.

Having a spatial location where punks can make something happen in their scenes has been both the motivating force and the glue that binds people at most volunteer-run spaces. "There's a book called *Free Spaces: The Sources of Democratic Change in America*, by Sara Evans and Harry Boyte, which I've often cited as a partial explanation for what happened at Gilman," Larry Livermore says to Amelia in an interview for the *MRR* website. "The book theorizes that for marginalized cultures to thrive and develop, people need a place where they can gather and work undisturbed and unobserved by the prying eyes and manipulating fingers of the dominant culture." Gilman is probably, along with ABC No Rio, one of the most often discussed community spaces. Gilman's affiliation with *MRR* has helped publicize the space in ways that distinguishes the Bay Area locale from others.

"Pretty much anyone could come there, start a band or an art project of some sort, and find, if not a receptive, at least a supportive audience," Larry says about Gilman. "But for at least the first couple years, almost no one knew about it except for other punks, artists, and weirdos. Because we had that little mini-world to operate in, we could develop our own ideas and expression without giving much thought to what the outside world might think or not think about us." That mini-world emerged because of the music, but, as Brian Edge notes in the introduction to *924 Gilman*, the people who "work the hardest and longest are the ones who find that 'rockin out' just isn't enough—there has to be more."

In most volunteer-run spaces anyone can become involved in multiple capacities. This openness is one of the key distinguishing features of these types of places and an important way that the spaces embody punk rock ideals. "Gilman continues to be a place that provides opportunities to people that can be found practically nowhere else. Where else could a sixteen-year-old be given a chance to run a club/community center on any given night?" writes Brian Edge in a January 1997 feature on the Gilman Street Project in *MRR*. "This place is run by people whose commitment and resolve have overcome lack of experience and skill." Many of the roadblocks that exist in mainstream music venues are absent from DIY spaces, where one of the more important guiding forces is simply a desire to participate and a willingness to help make something happen.

Of course, there are also many instances where people who are inexperienced or new to a scene need some guidance. Al Rios explains that at 1919 Hemphill in Fort Worth, Texas there are recurring efforts to recruit new volunteers, often starting with kids who are regular show participants, but who might not understand the inner-workings of show production. "And so, once they start volunteering we show 'em: this is how we book shows, and this is how we treat bands and pay bands, and this is what it takes to run a DIY space." Again, because volunteer-run spaces are explicitly politicized in ways that might not apply to houses (or some houses), mentoring will feature in these show spaces in ways that won't take shape in a house show scene. There are often multiple efforts by members of the volunteer-run spaces to encourage younger people to become more active rather than leaving everything to the older punks. At the same time, experience brings wisdom. "A band will play shows regularly or they'll be part of the scene or something and they'll do shit wrong or shit that I don't like and so I'll call them out on it: 'This is the way it should be for these reasons.' I'm really outspoken; I'm generally just an asshole. I make sure people know what I think. I've been around long enough that where I think that it means something. You know, that I know what I'm talking about so," Al says without completing the sentence while laughing.

When Brian Edge explains that a space like Gilman stands out because young punks can participate in the same ways as people who have been around the scene for some time, such opportunities exist not only because of mentoring but also because volunteer-run spaces seek to avoid the top-down management styles that limit creativity in bars and clubs. Chuck Munson writes in "Your Friendly Neighborhood Infoshop" in the January 1998 issue of *MRR* about the ways that most infoshops are set up to expand participation. Although infoshops usually have a broader focus than volunteer-run show spaces, both tend to adopt organizational models grounded in cooperative decision-making. "There is a tendency to gravitate towards using consensus to decide things, although this is not always the case. Needless to say, it is impossible to find an infoshop 'director' or 'president.'" Chuck writes that the decision to use membership models of governance can encourage greater commitment among a variety of volunteers, buffering against all of the work falling on the shoulders of a few people, but also "to make sure that not just anybody off the street could come in and vote."

Jeremy Smith explains to me that it took some time for the people who started Flywheel to arrive at a balance between collective participation and avoiding the stagnation and infighting that can occur if unanimous consent is required for decision-making. "We sort of went in with ideas about how it would work and then we had people taking advantage of it, people doing more work than others, certain shows being trouble shows. How do we make this space open for everyone to use but not jeopardize the future of the space?" Underground music spaces will require more negotiation among participants compared with other venues, where a top-down management system is ingrained into the culture. In bars and clubs, for example, employees understand that management will make decisions and others will follow. DIY spaces strive for more connection among participants, a greater sense of ownership for people involved, and to embody connections between politics and cultural life.

As I noted, Flywheel experienced some growing pains that were not unique to this Western Massachusetts space. On one hand, many punks are invested in making a scene where everyone has a voice. On the other hand, punks are used to calling people out when they think those folks have wronged the scene in some ways. Sometimes such actions can lead to stalemates, people quitting a project, or feelings of alienation. Such problems can lead to the undoing of a space because communal participation won't work if forgiveness is not going to be practiced. "It's always a balancing act. We realized quickly that the 'Hey man, be cool' philosophy wasn't gonna work out. Luckily we had some really good people that helped give us some organizational structure to make sure everyone was heard, give everyone opportunities," Jeremy notes, reflecting on some early crossroads faced by Flywheel's members. He adds that they struggled with getting bogged down by little things in part because people couldn't see beyond their own self-interests and make choices that would be best for the space.

Flywheel members also wrestled with tensions resulting from a desire to expand the space's scope and the products of such growth. Enlarging Flywheel's focus meant a more diverse membership became involved with the space. A more heterogeneous group coming to a project from different backgrounds and with varied goals can lead to increased disagreements. "We had some real strong soul searching," Jeremy remembers. "So when someone doesn't necessarily come from the same theme that we did, how do we make the space open to them? To not say, 'Oh, you don't believe what we believe, so you have to leave.' We really struggled with that."

One of the recurring themes in discourse surrounding the creation of a volunteer-run space is a desire to extend beyond punk shows. For example, some punks want to incorporate zine libraries, free classes/skillshares, community art programs, and/or opportunities for members of the local neighborhood to invest

PITF, Ranchos Huevos, Chicago, IL

themselves in the space. "We try not to typecast and/or be genre specific, which I think has been the downfall of many potentially great venues," JT Townsend tells Melissa Flanzraich about Charm City Art Space in Baltimore in an August 2003 *MRR* article. Mike Riley adds that Charm City was created to fill a number of DIY cultural needs in Baltimore, not just to function as a show space. "I think that most DIY venues run by punk/hardcore/indie kids seem to only focus on the music, and we are part of the minority that tries to bring in other forms of art." Such goals are respectable, and they have worked for Charm City since the space opened in 2002. But this success is also a product of Charm City expanding its focus within a doable framework: visual and performing arts, broadly speaking.

The range of possible activities that can take shape in a space will also be informed by the design of the space. Because volunteer-run spaces feel a bit more formal than a house, punks can do other punk-related activities there, which likely would seem out-of-place in a house environment where people expect to hear music and hang out. For example, Mess Hall was a self-described experimental cultural center in the Rogers Park neighborhood of Chicago, "a place where visual art, radical politics, creative urban planning, applied ecological design and other things intersect and inform each other." Mess Hall ran from 2003 until March 2013. It hosted some experimental sound art projects, but was not a recurring show space. But punk had a presence via a series called Hardcore Histories co-organized by Marc Fischer, Terence Hannum, and Paul Sargent. A discussion leader or a group of leaders developed the plans for a specific session and then created a program. I went to one session that was focused on Finnish hardcore and food was shared, whereas another program I attended focused on straight edge and was more of a lecture that mixed videos and music. A panel on women in punk featured conversation/Q&A and was followed by a music-listening session with different people taking turns as DJ.

Mess Hall had a policy that there were never entry fees (not even a donation-based system) and nothing was sold in the space, which would mean bands couldn't sell merch. Its organizers understood that such policies weren't good for bands but they "also felt like live music was fairly well covered [in Chicago], so that's not what this space needs to do," Marc explains. "But Mess Hall worked really well for discussion and for events that couldn't really find a home elsewhere." Marc and Terence hosted the first event; it focused on the seven-inch record format and what that meant for this kind of music, Marc remembers. "The first meal-related one we did was an Italian hardcore pasta dinner. People were encouraged to bring a dish or bring records." Marc notes that the co-organizers regularly discussed their goals for this series, especially since the rise of the Internet as a resource means that punks can easily find music from well-known and obscure locations. "But collectively people were bringing in this stuff, so you could have a tactile experience with stuff that is dispersed across many homes. And at this Italian dinner people brought in this really rare stuff that I had been dying to hear but that you would never have time to listen to all of it but here it was like, 'Yeah put it on.'" He adds that it was amazing that anyone could find out about the event in *The Reader* (Chicago's alternative weekly) and if they were even mildly curious, they could show up to Mess Hall for good conversation. Normally "you would have to know a person who knew a person to be able to see this stuff [the actual records] but here some 40-year-old could share records with a fifteen-year-old, who knew nothing about it. So this kind of education could happen."

We expect music spaces to function in a specific fashion. Even though a punk house models a transformed use of space, punks don't expect to find a public lecture in a basement. However, people have much broader expectations for volunteer-run spaces because such places have histories of doing more than hosting shows. Of course, working out the nuances of programming within these community sites isn't always easy.

Chuck Munson's descriptions of finding the proper balance with participation and programming in infoshops offer a nice parallel to volunteer-run punk spaces. Chuck writes that if infoshops rely too heavily on the punk scene, such spaces can benefit from the energy that punks bring to a project, but "punks are, by and large, transient youth. Like many young people, they have a wide range of interests and tend to move around a lot. They aren't settled members of the community so they may perceive that the project will carry on if they leave." Again, the parallel to newly forming DIY spaces would be a struggle between taking stock of punk's ephemeral features, knowing that a place run by punks can run hot and then burn out, yet trying to extend the reach beyond punk can mean that participants don't share enough interests to see the project through. One person wants a daycare program, another wants a music education program, someone else is interested in working on an initiative to secure books for prisoners, and all of them can't stand punk.

This last problem featured early in ABC No Rio's history. In the March 1994 issue of *MRR*, the ABC Collective writes in an article for the magazine: "For years it was touch-and-go whether the shows would continue, as the artists fought with the city over the lease and looked down their noses at us. By last year it had, however, become clear that the matinee shows were the only event bringing in any money." The ABC Collective notes that the artists quit and the punks took over, inheriting the building and the lease. This would change again, as implied in the discussion of ABC No Rio earlier in the chapter. But at one point in ABC No Rio's important history punks did not fit into the plans of people who were running No Rio. Thus, as with renting city spaces or veterans halls, the relationships between punks and other groups can be tenuous. By the punks and for the punks will at least offer a common starting point for a space. This was the approach adopted by the ABC Collective when they took over. "Anyone can participate, and about a dozen regulars make up the core group, which has no officers. In order to vote, you have to attend three meetings in the past three months." They write that meetings last for hours, "which tends to discourage the most active/busiest punx from attending." Turnout at the sessions ranges "from a handful to several dozen."

Jeremy notes that they responded to some of the difficulties at Flywheel by changing the by-laws and the criteria for becoming a member of the voting body. Volunteers who want to vote on policies go through an interview process and others who prefer to help out/book shows but not join the voting body would be supported as well. Other than a hiatus while Flywheel moved from its first space to the larger current space, it has been running since March 1999. This solid history is a product of having a clear system for decision-making combined with a focused identity:

a space for live performance-related activities (music, poetry/ spoken word, film and video screenings), meetings, discussion groups, and a zine library.

Melanie Losover describes a similar combination of clear purpose and participatory structure at Charm City Art Space. She tells me that that the decision-making process has been the same since she joined in 2009. That stability is important, she argues. "We're a collective; everyone weighs in on decisions regarding the space. We have meetings and people can vote or people vote through our email listserv." Melanie observes that the only real difference between the time when she started volunteering and now is the people (some have drifted away and others have joined), although there is stability on that front as well. "We've had the same seven people involved that have probably been involved for as long as I have and longer and then there will be new people who come in. Generally, we get a new member every month or every two months. Some people will join and become really involved; they'll become another voice we'll hear when we're making decisions. There are people who will join just so they feel like they can be part of it and they will be vocal sometimes and maybe become more participatory later."

Al Rios tells me that at any given time 1919 has ten to twelve volunteers who regularly participate in the running of the space, with a few others helping out here and there. The volunteers who are most active live near the space, whereas those who are peripherally involved tend to live farther away. "Most of the decisions are made through consensus. The little everyday bullshit we trust each other enough to get it done," Al says. He adds that they are at a transitional point because a lot of the work had fallen on the shoulders of one guy named Rick. Rick was handling the day-to-day business decisions and was around every night to help oversee shows. But then he left, which Al claims, created a big hole. "Any time any hard decision needed to get made and nobody knew what to do, we all looked at Rick for his sage advice. And now that he's not there, that vacuum I'm filling. Mostly because I'm a pompous blowhard." Al adds that he's trying to prevent a similar situation where one person is relied on to do most of the work, so he finds himself delegating more often, letting volunteers know about various projects or tasks and then encouraging these members to figure it out. Not only does being able to delegate spread the workload but such efforts also help foster commitment to 1919. "When it existed for the first few years it was always this really, 'Who knows if it's going to be there tomorrow. Who knows if it's gonna last.' And now it's like an institution; it's set, we're there. All the kids.....most of the kids that are volunteers, 1919 has been there the entire time that they've been a punk, so they don't know the world without 1919; they don't know DFW [Dallas–Fort Worth] without 1919. And so they, I don't want to say they take it for granted, but there's no sense of urgency or caution or being scared shitless of us one day being run out by the landlord because our neighborhood is being gentrified and maybe our rent is going to triple. They're just kind of like, 'Well, it's been there for so long; it's gonna be there.' And so the bigger decisions that need to be made, they don't see it with the same level of panic that I do because I'm still in the mode of 'This could be gone tomorrow.' So, they're just kind of like, 'I don't know whatever you think.' And I'm like, 'Nooooo! I'm old. I don't have good ideas anymore,'" he says, laughing.

The organizational politics extend to the ways that volunteer-run spaces work with bands. Al Rios explains to me that 1919 usually caps shows at $5 for local bands and $6 if there is a touring band. He says that they only go above $6 if the bill is filled with touring bands and that has only happened a few times since he started booking there. The space opened in 2002 and that length of operation has allowed the volunteers to develop a better sense of 1919's finances. They don't have a hard and fast rule when it comes to dividing money, as was the case when the place first opened. Now they understand what they need to keep going and then do the best they can for the touring bands. "Lately we've gotten smarter and more reasonable about it. We used to do even splits. Say there's two out-of-town bands, so we'd do 1/3, 1/3, 1/3. If we make $300, it would be $100, $100, $100. That was when we weren't having so many shows, so we needed to get more money from shows. Lately we'll have fifteen shows a month, so we don't need $100 from each show. So, every show we'll just look at where we are that month, how many people came, if there were a bunch of people for the out-of-town bands versus the local band, and then all the volunteers will talk, and we'll be like, 'Ok, we're gonna keep $50 and we're gonna give them $150 or whatever.'" He says that they rarely pay local bands unless the show makes a lot of money and the local band is hurting for gas money. Mostly, Al notes, when they've tried to pay local bands, those bands tell 1919 bookers to keep the money; the bands understand that 1919 needs the money more than the local bands need the funds.

Melanie explains that Charm City's landlord and the city are aware of the space's focus, but it is not a legal venue, and this status affects how they manage show costs. "We can't say you have to pay this amount to get in, so we say, 'requested donation.' Generally it ranges from $5 to $10 depending on what the promoter wants to do. We do have benefit shows for the space and sometimes for other causes. And sometimes we have free shows. In order to pay the space the promoter either does $60 or one-third, whichever is higher. So basically it has to get to $60 and after that we have a chart that shows increments. It's up to the promoter to decide how they want to divide it amongst bands. Let's say a show doesn't do so well and they don't have the $60 to pay, they can owe that $60 and pay it back at a later date. They don't have to pay it that night if they want to pay the bands."

The general approach to running these DIY spaces often filters to the experience of attending shows there, both positively and negatively. Al Rios compares 1919 to Dave's, which is a house in Denton. He reiterates that 1919 is a sober space, but they are located in the middle of a neighborhood with a lot of liquor stores and some people will end up drinking prior to a show. "If I was gonna have a pop punk show at 1919 versus Dave's, it would be way more chill at 1919. Way rowdier at Dave's." But others explain to me that the DIY focus of house spaces and volunteer-run spaces transcends the spatial nuances of each; both feel similar. And another group might be clustered around the idea of supporting a volunteer-run DIY space. That is, they acknowledged that a house show feels different than a volunteer-run space but prefer the latter because attending shows or playing at such spaces is both an economic and embodied commitment to the cultural politics of such spaces. For example, Ramy Silyan from the band Ten Thousand Leagues, tells me about his early efforts booking shows in LA. "I started doing this because I had no other options. Then I think with Hyde Park Half [a community space that he helped found in Inglewood, California], having group meetings and a collective, then I got into: 'Well, how do you feel? What do you think?' We were all talking about what we all think is the best way to do this show." In other words, he went from doing DIY by himself to doing DIY as a political act that could be enacted collectively.

In general, the volunteer-run place is going to be better organized than a house, the physical space will usually be larger and cleaner (although Ramy jokes that Hyde Park Half was a shoebox of a space: long and narrow), and that expanse and cleanliness allows for other politicized and communal opportunities (e.g., tables for political projects and zines, potlucks, large enough area for band merch). Volunteer-run spaces will also move from one location to another to best maximize the total space available for members. For example, Flywheel and Charm City both moved from their original locations to larger spaces because they needed more room given the amount of people who were attending shows and other events. I have never heard of anyone moving to a larger house because the house could not contain the number of people attending shows that were being hosted. Any move from one house to another is tied to a quest for cheaper rent or basically being evicted. Moreover, the collective politics of a volunteer-run space filters through the ways that punks then infuse the space and can inform the types of bands that play there. Many of the first volunteer-run spaces would examine a band's lyrics before deciding to book the band.

The successes experienced by volunteer-run spaces also come with disappointments. In *924 Gilman* Tim Yohannan said in an interview with Hawk that some of the original plans to experiment with the experience of doing shows failed to materialize. "One of our first policies was that we weren't going to announce who was playing," Tim said. The punks involved with Gilman wanted people to support the space rather than showing up only when a specific band was of interest. They also "had bands help work the shows in order to play there. The whole point of the place was to try and create, or further, an alliance between participants and bands to run the place together." He noted that this idea also failed. "If we didn't announce who was playing, people didn't come. Bands didn't want to work, and did so only grudgingly."

A genealogy of punk rock discourse highlights how the volunteer-run space is a kind of magical ideal for punks, which was expressed in Tim's hopes that Gilman could be something more than a DIY mirror of a mainstream club. There is a steady-flow of proclamations in various scenes about new volunteer-run spaces being formed and similar claims published in fanzines. It's understandable why punks want to create these spaces. Volunteer-run spaces should in theory provide an alternative to the unsteady house show scene and problems with official city parks and community spaces. Moreover, unlike a house, which is almost always going to be tied to an individual or a small group renting the house and then dies off when the renters move out (minus the rare exceptions), the volunteer-run space should be able to change with a changing scene. For example, the people who helped found Gilman, Charm City, and 1919 are no longer running those spaces, yet each is thriving.

Many punks don't realize, though, that starting a "legitimate" or "above ground" DIY space comes with responsibilities that can be way more emotionally and financially draining than a house. The volunteer-run space just shifts the difficulties that accompany a house show space and then adds new ones. For every success story, there are hundreds of volunteer-run spaces that either never got off the ground or burned out quickly. Of course, all of these spaces, even the ones that don't last long, model that big things are possible on a small scale.

Managing the bureaucratic maze established by local governments is perhaps the principal problem for people trying to open a DIY space. Tim Yohannan discussed this in *924 Gilman*, explaining that the crew that started the Gilman Project in 1986 was naïve about the difficulties that surround opening such a space. "Eight months of paying rent on the place before we could even open, and investing over $40,000 in the place for rent, construction, etc., also before we could open. Also there was a huge amount of red tape, hearings with the city, inspections by health, fire, police, etc."

That amount of money required to get Gilman going could have paralyzed the participants. Luckily there were enough resources in the Bay Area, and *MRR's* involvement helped bring together a variety of punks who understood the importance of volunteerism given the magazine's reliance on volunteer labor. But other punks have faced similar pressures and could not keep their spaces open. For example, Vic Vicars tells me that the end of Ghost House inspired the creation of Mad Ave in Lincoln, Nebraska. "There were a handful of shows that last summer of 2011 where there were a lot bigger bands, whether it was dumb luck or we just happened to be friends with whoever at that point that wanted to play the house," says Vic about Ghost House. "Our house wasn't big enough to hold everything that was happening." The size of these shows led to police appearing regularly and threatening to issue fines that were beyond what people in the house could afford. "We needed something more sustainable. This house had done what we needed it to do for a long time but maybe what we have created, which I was very proud of at that time, was this community of people (and I'm still in touch with many of them) and we had created something that was a lot bigger than four years ago."

Vic and some of his friends decided that the best move was to find a space that could meet their DIY needs while avoiding problems with noise violations and potential fines tied to minors consuming alcohol at the house; they started working on Mad Ave. Right away, though, they learned how different things are when doing a so-called legitimate space compared to the chaotic freedom of a house show. "We landed on our face so hard and were thousands of dollars in debt because of this space. Instead of this crappy non-OSHA compliant basement with these rickety stairs, we have to go to the city and get permits, fire escapes, and all this stuff." It's one thing to do shows in one's house and figure out how to make the space work, but it's another thing to navigate a system of legal codes that don't make sense to the average person. "None of us were building planners. None of us were pre-law. We didn't understand how a lot of this stuff works. We rented this building and it worked great and then 'No, no, no.'"

Vic notes that they were making this move knowing that people in the scene were excited about DIY music, as evidenced in the fact that the final shows at Ghost House drew more people than the house could hold. Vic also acknowledges that "If you've been in DIY punk long enough, you know that with any community or scene there are people who have come before you, so you build off of what they have established to continue growing." Vic speaks to the point I raised above about some punks now relying on more established DIY spaces as models for creating a local show space. Understanding that others have built something successful is important, since such spaces serve as role models. However, the stability of one space doesn't guarantee the longevity of spaces that follow, nor does it mean that one can do a one-to-one transfer of lessons learned since each city has its own unique roadblocks.

"We thought in our mind that we were doing the right thing by going to city: This is what we're doing. What do you think about this?" Vic remembers. "We hear: 'You don't have the right number of bathrooms. You don't have fire protection stuff: a sprinkler system, a extinguisher, the door has to be going in instead of out.' Then we had to get all these people from the city to come. We put in the sprinkler system and built the handicap-accessible bathroom and we now thought we were in compliance. We were told: 'It's good that you did these things.' But then the police chief comes and he says, 'No. No. No. I think this is dangerous.' We meet with this stereotypical movie police chief: 'What happens if this happens?' And 'You have this one handicapped-accessible bathroom,' which was approved by the Board of Public Works. 'What happens if you have 70 people and they all need to use the bathroom? A bunch of them cross the street to use the bathroom at the gas station and one of them gets hit by a car.' That's why we have insurance." Vic says that the whole situation felt as if the police chief didn't want the space to happen so they described every minor issue as a potential life-threatening problem.

Eventually, the group jumped through all the hoops, but then new problems appeared. "We do shows for a while and the cops would come and claim that we had a disturbance complaint from another business. It's eight at night and there aren't any other businesses open. It just seemed like they were making a case out of nothing. Eventually our landlord got worried about what might or might not be happening in this space, which was drug and alcohol-free. So he said, 'Look guys, I'm sorry but I'm going to have to shut you down.'" They stopped doing Ghost House in the summer of 2011, and by autumn 2011 Mad Ave was closed. Even that small window of time was inconsistent, given these external pressures. The Facebook site for Mad Ave lists some shows happening and some being moved to other spaces.

Ramy tells a similar story about Hyde Park Half. They "would have the cops show up every now and again and the cops were actually surprisingly really nice," he explains to me. "I remember once they showed up I immediately shut the door. You know I wouldn't give them consent to come in and I would meet them halfway down the block and I'd be like, 'All right, so look this is what's going on. I'm having a show down there; this is a community space. We're not drinking, we're not doing drugs, and everyone's gonna go home.' Looking back, it's almost like I told them what's gonna happen and that's what happened," he says. "Then I told them that they could come in. I told everyone, 'Hey, I'm letting these cops in. I have to or else the show's not going to happen.' And everyone agreed. We let them take a look inside." Ramy says that the cops were mostly concerned about drugs and alcohol, but Hyde Park Half was a sober space, so there were no problems with the police. "Ultimately, we got shut down by the Fire Marshall because it was a firetrap. There was no backdoor and the only door that went out was a door built in the '20s that swung in. And the shows were literally wall-to-wall. This place was tiny."

Everyone I interviewed who is (or was) affiliated with a volunteer-run space, talked about the challenges faced trying to keep the space running. Even long-running, seemingly successful places faced such challenges. Similarly, conversations regularly focused on people in the scene policing the spaces. Problems with fights or any kind of violence was exceptionally rare. This ability by punks to consistently create safe spaces throughout the country foregrounds the irony of city officials working to undermine or shutdown volunteer-run DIY spaces. These officials are so worried about what kids will do under the influence of punk rock music, but problems rarely exist in small spaces. Instead, the large venues, the places that various local governments support, are locations where people act like fools. If kids want to see shows in many cities, they have no choice but to attend large venues, which can model brutality, and they rarely display how punk rock community is enacted. Moreover, most volunteer-run spaces are sober spaces, which can limit problems that take shape in these other locations. Melanie notes that Charm City has "always been no drugs, no alcohol. Not even outside the space." She adds that this policy is crucial to the longevity of the space. "The police know we're not gonna have kids drinking outside the space, underage drinking, or otherwise."

After shows stopped at the Bike House, Jenny Ray started booking at the Pheonix Project, a volunteer-run community/art space in Dallas, which is now known as 406. "There is just no better feeling than having a band come through, you have a great show, and everyone has a great time. There's a good amount of money and you're able to put 'em up and everyone's just like, 'Yeaaaaaaaah.' It makes me feel great inside," she tells me. "I wanted to keep doing it, but sometimes it gets hard because you feel like you are one of the only people who do that. There aren't a lot of people in North Texas who are booking. Sometimes it gets hard because you feel like a lot of people rely on you. You can't rely on one person, man. You've got to have other people." The advantage of most volunteer-run spaces is that one person isn't doing everything, although work imbalance can happen over time. Working collectively can help insure a space's survival by providing a buffer against the transience of some punks. Moreover, spreading the workload can ease the pressure that can be felt if one person is responsible for most of the booking (as Jenny describes). Jen Angel reiterates this last point in the first of a three-part series she wrote for *MRR*: "A Beginners Guide to Putting on Shows." She notes in the November 1994 issue: "The first thing you will need is help. Yes, it is possible to do shows by yourself, but it's never as much fun, and it's always more work and frustrating for you. So get all your friends to help." Many established volunteer-run spaces have adopted this approach through a formalized system where volunteers learn how to run the sound, work the door, and help out with a variety of other needs (which might include working a café/small counter for food and beverages). Once the volunteers learn how to do these various jobs, they can join a rotating three-person crew, which includes the promoter for the specific show. Again, such collective efforts can help avoid burnout while reaffirming an invitational approach to doing DIY together/integrating punks into the community.

Although there are people in houses who will share the work, most house shows are handled by the person who books the show. Chris Moore tells me that he sometimes receives help when he books in Washington, DC "But I'd say that most of the time I do everything myself. I make the food, make the flyer, flyer for it, I've bought multiple PAs over the years. I don't fuckin' sing. I shouldn't have to buy a PA, but I have two now." The product of doing it himself is that Chris limits the amount of shows he books because "I feel like the more I do, the less effort I can put into them. I feel bad taking on a show that I really, really can't put a lot of work into."

Chris describes choices he makes that are guided by a general sense of responsibility to fellow punks. But not everyone approaches punk shows in the same way. Tony Gravedigger from the Bay Area band The Gravediggers writes a letter to *MRR* in June 1996 to call out the decision-makers at Gilman after a Gilman member had argued that The Gravediggers would "bring an unwanted element to Gilman and a new band night will be an inappropriate show for that considering Mothers, Fathers, Aunts and Uncles often frequent these shows." Tony responds that the band's following mostly consists of "street punks & non-racist skins" and challenges the changes as he sees them at Gilman: "In my opinion, it's bad enough that Gilman is overrun with rich trendoid alternateens, but fuck, now we have to cater to their 'Mothers, Fathers, Aunts and Uncles' as well? I remember when punks used to come from broken homes and seek out safe havens away from their families." It is certainly easier to complain about the ways that a space runs than to volunteer at that space and try to usher in changes. In this case, The Gravediggers could have found another venue to play if the politics of Gilman weren't in line with their cultural politics, but Tony Gravedigger's letter foregrounds the ways that not everyone will be happy with what is happening within a space. The challenge for the volunteer-run space will be to decide how a space can expand to be more inclusive or when such broadening of shows will undermine the space's mission.

Other punks avoid volunteer-run spaces in general, showing no interest in helping to establish such spaces, which is what happened in Chicago a few years back when members of DIYCHI were trying to organize a collective effort to start a volunteer-run space. Basically, many of the most vocal punks responsible for booking some of Chicago's longer running houses felt that there were enough houses going and that houses were a much better option for punk shows since all of the money goes to touring bands. These punks were quick to accuse DIYCHI of taking money out of bands' pockets via the pipedream of a DIY space. "There was a lot of pushback because we were getting money from the shows but we were being really transparent about it," says Matt Walsh. "We're taking $50, and not at every show. We're taking $50 when we're paying the bands $300." He says that people who were most critical of DIYCHI were already established and felt as if they didn't need anyone's help. "The thing is that the people who were coming to meetings weren't the same people that were coming to shows. They were looking to do something different but they would come to a show or two and then drop off." Matt's hope was that different people would join the collective who had something to bring (i.e., at the time he had a house that could be used for shows, and he hoped someone would join that had experience with laws, or construction skills, or had worked on grants). "That was the thing, to most people it was just weirdos trying to do something; it wasn't the top dogs of punk. If a bunch of different people would have shown up, that would have gotten it moving." The shitstorm on the forums increased, Alderaan had to stop doing shows, and Matt says he became disillusioned. There is another effort to found a DIY space in Chicago, but the early energies seem to have been met with the spatial-economic realities of trying to open a place.

I understand why a vibrant house show network excites so many punks, both from economic and experiential standpoints. However, the constant fear of houses being shut down, the difficulty guaranteeing shows for bands when there are only a few houses, and the radical deviation in types of show spaces (e.g., how late the show can run) all limit promoters. Then there's the issue of offering a realistic all-ages option for teenagers who are young enough that their parents will want to know about the shows being attended.

Grace Ambrose writes in her December 2014 *MRR* column about going to shows when she was in high school. Her parents allowed her to see bands any night of the week as long as she earned straight A's in school. "I spent all of my money and most of my spare time going to gigs," she writes. She was a regular at well-known club spaces (9:30 Club and Black Cat), college campus shows, and "occasionally houses. I didn't tell them about the houses (parents, *maaaan*, they don't get it) but I told them about pretty much everything else." She doesn't say why she would not tell them about houses, but the "man, they don't get it" comment speaks to the logical rationale: parents are likely to assume that the house show is a raging party. They will presume that if bands are playing at a house, the parents who live in the house are out-of-town. If the kid can explain that there aren't parents, because, say, college students rent the house, then the parents are going to be more freaked out. As Lily from Parasol MA says to me, "I think that community spaces are so awesome. You can put an address on the flyer. You're telling your mom you are going to the Democracy Center and not some wackadoo house in Alston. My mom would have much rather dropped me off there at sixteen than at someone's house."

Melanie notes that Charm City's fixed address and identity was crucial for her ability to integrate into the scene there as a high school kid. "I probably started going to shows at the Art Space when I was maybe fifteen [or] sixteen; I was in high school. That was my introduction to DIY. In 2009 I decided to join the Art Space and start booking shows. I didn't see a lot of the shows that I wanted to go and see happening. I wanted to be the one to make those shows happen. I wanted to be part of it because I could tell, from going to the Art Space, that there was a tight sense of community there. Everyone was friends and that was something that was important to me; I wanted to get more involved and meet new people." Melanie says that she lived in Baltimore her entire life, and most of her friends in school shared interests other than music. She was trying to find another crew that was into music. She's been booking shows at Charm City for five years and feels as if that same connection wouldn't have been possible for a high school teen without a volunteer-run space.

Melanie adds that a lot of kids find their way to Charm City in the same way she did. "People who have their parents drop off are attending the shows. I think it's also that we have a website.

You can look us up on a map and say, 'Here mom. This place is legitimate. This is where I'm going.' Whereas for a house show: 'I can't really show you anything because it's someone's house' and their parents might not be so ok with that. But they see on our website: no drinking, no drugs, all-ages. It's a very friendly, welcoming environment and they might feel more ok with it."

Volunteer-run spaces are built with the idea that more people need to join. Again, the model is not to hide ("ask a punk") but instead to be invitational in focus. The volunteer-run space will likely face a need to remain relevant in ways that won't apply

Libyans, 05/21/10, Fucking Discovery Zone, New Haven, CT

to a house, since houses aren't expected to be sustained and most will close before people can grow tired of the space. But volunteer-run spaces emerge because punks in a scene believe that their geographical area needs an all-ages, punk-controlled space. The space can be big, it can be small, it can be well-known in punk circles or only known among punks in a certain part of the country, but eventually the space will struggle. At this point, punks will have to confirm a commitment to making the space last, which is what happened with ABC No Rio, with Gilman, and with the Mr. Roboto Project.

"The Roboto Project really signals a big change in Pittsburgh," Mike Seamans tells me. "It was a DIY music venue, drug and alcohol free, and unlike these house venues it was run with the intention of being a show space to do any kind of music but it was started as a punk/hardcore space. There were shows three or four nights a week for almost ten years." Roboto is one of the success stories in the U.S., functioning as a show space, providing a basement location for bands to practice, and serving as a space for members to start a bike co-op (which has since moved to its own space). Mike adds, though, that the space's highs (drawing 100+ kids on a Thursday night) have also been met with some lows. "Pittsburgh went through a bit of a decline. There just weren't a lot of new kids coming into the scene; it stagnated a little bit." He notes that punks his age (early 30s) started buying homes in parts of the city that weren't as close to Roboto. "They have more regular jobs or whatever. And going over to Wilkinsburg for a show just seemed to be less and less appealing. Also, since it didn't seem like that many kids were going to shows, the shows started to move to bars. And another thing that happened about the same time is all of these art galleries and other venue spaces started to open in Pittsburgh that were slightly more convenient locations and less and less shows started happening at Roboto."

Mike says that Roboto closed for about a year and then re-opened in a new location that's on the same strip as the art galleries. "Now I am seeing that there are more and more kids coming and suddenly I am seeing high school kids coming to shows again. And that's awesome," claims Mike. "Where my record store is, and the neighborhood where I've lived for the last seven years, there's a bar that does shows and I would be putting shows together and would think, 'I'm just gonna do it at the bar because it's convenient, it's easy, people show up, and it's packed out. I felt bad that some kids missed the shows but the last all-ages shows I did there would only be one or two kids that came." But Mike decided to do his next show at Roboto and was excited to see that "there were a ton of kids that came. That was sort of a surprise."

In the end, the volunteer-run space can provide greater opportunities for punks to help shape their scenes. The spaces are material reflections of collectivist ideologies and identity politics. Many punks feel as if these spaces explicitly invite participation and others attribute their growth as people and as punks to experiences in these spaces. For example, one of the local kids, A.J., who booked some shows at Roboto, says in the *Building a Better Robot* book that he was changed by the political climate of Roboto. "I will say that the space was directly responsible for my cessation of using the word 'faggot.' Despite never having ill feelings toward anyone of a different sexual persuasion, the power of what I thought at the time to be a simple word was never called into question [until I saw it] brought into conversation at Roboto." A house can have a similar influence, but the time and space for political conversations are rarely built into the house show experience. Instead, such spaces tend to focus more directly on shows and the bands. I believe scenes need both types of DIY spaces (and others if the scene can support more). There is great political value in creating a space that also serves as a public face for local punk, but it's nice to have a more chaotic complement in the form of a healthy house show scene. This blend of political engagement and raw energy reflects the sounds and the scenes that make punk a distinct music and culture but also a diverse music and culture.

Section IV

What We Do Should Not Be Secret

Raw Nerve, Last Show, 4/14/12, Mousetrap, Chicago, IL

New Noise for $5

The Impalers are working their way through a blistering set at Mousetrap. They move quickly from one song to the next, without much break in between. This is the way things should go: twenty minutes of pure energy and that's that. Time to relax for a few minutes while the next band sets up and the experience repeats with a different sound. A band member's monologue between each song might last longer than the songs, and by the end of the set we've heard ten minutes of music and fifteen minutes of proselytizing. Other bands fly through their set in a more worker bee fashion, stopping momentarily to tune (usually one guitarist tunes while a second guitar produces a sea of feedback). This has been the approach adopted by The Impalers. Whether bands stop to talk or fly through their set, we experience something unique and then the moment passes, not to return again. We can see the same band at the same house on a future date but the encounter will be different. The crowd will change. New songs will be played. Band members will organize themselves in the space in a different fashion. But I say all of this knowing that so much of punk's "you had to be there" qualities have increasingly developed a second life through a variety of media.

For punks of a certain age, *The Decline of the Western Civilization* is a crucial visual touchstone for understanding punk rock in a particular time and place. The film footage found in its still photography complements that in photozines (e.g., Glen E. Friedman's *My Rules*) and the photos on album covers (e.g., Minor Threat on the back of the *Flex Your Head* comp). Changes in punk can be traced through images presented in records and zines: the front cover of the DYS *Wolfpack* album to the front and back covers of Youth of Today's *Break Down the Walls*. A few years on and we witness a major sea change, with the iconic images of Riot Grrrl bands and a proliferation of documented show spaces modeling how spastic energy can be exuded in a communal fashion. Such approaches informed the emotive hardcore bands that were forming throughout the U.S. in the early-to-mid 1990s. Some bands sought to mirror a style that was happening with the fashionable focus of Nation of Ulysses (even if the sounds of were more directly linked to the Nation of Ulysses' more famous labelmates, Fugazi.)

The rapid emergence of prosumer video cameras, which further developed into contemporary high quality HD video cameras/DSLRs, has meant that more people can document punk rock experiences. Now it is possible to search YouTube to find footage of both well-known and obscure bands playing DIY spaces. We can see early shows at Gilman, bands playing at Lost Cross, sets from the short window when Hyde Park Half was running, and thousands of bands playing at other DIY spaces. The media content starts to blend together after a while. That is, video footage of Comadre at Hyde Park Half shows a more diverse scene than the shot of Minor Threat on the back cover of *Flex Your Head*, but the chaos of a singer engulfed in a crowd of punks looks very similar. And the audiences always seem to be the same age. Punk rock has a Neverland quality about it, perpetually young. In fact, other than the Dropdead show at Democracy Center, seeing Los Crudos at ChiTown Futbol in 2013, and sporadic basement shows that include a band that features someone who has been in the scene a long time, I am usually guaranteed to be the oldest punk in the room. The general experience of the scene stays the same but the people who make the scene continually recycle. This is a major contributing factor to the why DIY house spaces do not last. But as one group of punks drift away from show spaces, new punks figure out what to do. Amidst all of the chopping and changing, two features seem to hold strong: a quest to find a creative outlet where punks can do DIY shows and belief that shows should cost $5.

• • •

Boxing posters line the walls behind the Danish post-punk band Iceage. The band's rhythm section builds to a noisy groove, and the guitar joins the thick sound. Elias, the band's singer, has a style that is part slur and part growl. He leans into the mic stand, rocks back and forth, and sways from side to side. The band is engulfed by people who bob their heads. Some jump up and down when the song speeds up during the chorus, a sort of post-punk breakdown. But there really isn't much room to move in the sixteen- to twenty-square-foot space. The band is playing inside a boxing ring at Munoz Gym in Bakersfield.

Ronald Ramirez, who owns Going Underground Records, explains to me that he needed a space after the basement of Jerry's, a local pizza shop that was the main spot for punk shows, had become off limits for Ronald and some of his friends. "We did the first show at the gym in 1998," he tells me. "What happened is that we got banned from Jerry's. We had been banned a couple times because we were young and stupid so when we would play we were young and stupid, wild and breaking shit. We were into Antioch Arrow and stuff like that so were trying to be crazy. Basically they fuckin' banned us for the last time, so 'Fuck you, we'll do our own shows.' And that's what we did. So I asked my grandpa, 'Can we use your gym to do a show?' And he said, 'Why would you want to do a show in there? It's too small.' 'Well, just let me do it.' And he said 'Ok, but don't mess it up.' We've messed it up, of course, over the years."

The space is still a functioning gym, although not super-active. "There's a ring, a couple hit bags and a speed bag; everything is in this one room. It's real small. He used to do a chicken egg business and so originally the boxing gym is where they used to keep the chickens. So after he closed up the chicken operation, he would do the gym and manage boxers; that's where everyone would train." Ronald explains that shows don't happen in this space too frequently because he understands that the gym is not in the best shape and he also tries to book shows that will be interesting for people, trying to avoid burnout by having too many bands play too often.

Some punks have the passion and a knack for finding a way to carve out a place where shows can happen, and those are the people who help a scene come alive. For example, Dan Dittmer explains that there were some houses used for shows in Rapid City, South Dakota but the houses tended not to last. Instead, he had better luck working with a variety of rotating places where he could do all-ages shows: banquet rooms at the local Howard Johnson's or Day's Inn, a pool hall, and a VFW Hall. "I even did a show at the 4H building on the fairgrounds. That was Dead Silence and Green Day. It's like we just missed the sheep auction, it's Dead Silence and Green Day, and the next day is the llama exhibit or whatever. Minus the smell, it was a great place."

The creative effort is at the core of doing DIY. I have already discussed how such labor is applied in the context of house shows and volunteer-run spaces. Much of that analysis was preceded by an exploration of early DIY efforts among punks throughout the U.S. to find a range of official (e.g., VFW halls) and unofficial spaces to play (e.g., stalled housing developments). But there are other types of spaces that fall somewhere between the house and the volunteer-run space that deserve a brief mention. Ronald's shows at Munoz gym fit that bill. Similarly, shows that Mike Swiatlowski booked for about two years at The Old Store in Palmer, Massachusetts also reflect a DIY spirit but did not happen at a more common space.

The Old Store was an old pharmacy that was owned by Mike's grandfather before his grandfather retired. Mike's parents still owned the building when Mike and his friends started doing shows there. Thus, The Old Store was ultimately Mike's project (akin to a house), but everything happened in partnership with other punks and the space was centrally located in Palmer's business district. The efforts of Mike and his friends offer a lot of insights into struggles punks can face when trying to do shows in a small town, especially when such shows happen in the heart of downtown. His labors also highlight that problems with local governments aren't exclusive to volunteer-run spaces.

When Mike's show at the American Legion hall fell through, his parents encouraged him to do the show in the store. Mike and his friends only needed to clear out the shelving and other junk that had been left behind when the pharmacy closed, or so they thought. The hard part was dealing with the town's officials. Mike notes that they had to jump through a lot of hoops to make shows happen, most of which were tied to the town's requirement for an entertainment license. Palmer officials were treating shows at the Old Store as akin to music at a bar. "I used to go to the board of selectmen meetings in town to ask for permission to do these shows. They made me do this little dog and pony show and ask for permission. But we didn't know any better, so if that's what it took to put on a show then that's what we did." It's important to stress that Mike was eighteen years old and most of the other kids helping put on the shows were fifteen or sixteen years old, so appearing in front of board members was certainly a nerve-wracking experience. The selectmen were concerned about safety, so they ordered that Mike meet with a building inspector (which luckily did not lead to many big repair costs) and they mandated security. "We had to rent a police officer to stand outside. That was our biggest expense, like $150 a night."

The upside to the use of this space was the lack of rental fees. Their only internal expense was paying the electric bill, which Mike says was really cheap. The cost for the cop was basically akin to the fee on a community hall. But they were also stuck with the expense because officials (like the managers at the American Legion hall) were freaked out about punk shows. "Everybody expected us to be doing something wrong, but really we just weren't. I always said that if we have to have a cop, they stay outside. We police the stuff inside," Mike explains to me. "There was such a big crowd of us who knew that this thing was so fragile that one slip-up (someone caught drinking in the back or one fight) it would have been done and over. We never would have been able to do this again. A lot of people were looking out for the space itself." Mike adds that he and John Boilard have probably done over 200 shows at The Old Store, The Shed, and other spaces they have booked and during that time have never had any major incidents. "I'm proud of that. We watch out for each other. We were sort of misfits in a way because we weren't tough guys, but we were smart about what we were doing."

They didn't have problems with the police officer, but some nights that could have been troublesome. "We had Converge play in '99 or 2000 and we had almost 400-500 kids. This was one night luckily when a police officer couldn't make it because we were well over capacity. We knew that we were inviting this band and what type of fans were capable of showing up, but we didn't have any problems. It was packed and it was wild, but no fights. Nothing like that. Again, there were so many people watching out to make sure that kind of stuff didn't happen."

This type of community-focused responsibility can be an amazing feature of punk scenes. Unfortunately, some places lack those social connections. "Here, that spirit to start a DIY non-profit does not exist," Cameron Cisneros tells me about Orange County, California. "Unit B [skate park] is cool but it's a business. It's not by the kids for the kids; it's by the adults for the kids." Cameron co-owns Mass Media Records with his wife Tricia, which is a label and a distro that focuses primarily on dark punk/goth/ death rock/anarcho punk. They also owned a record store for a few years, where they would host one to two shows per month out of their Santa Ana location. Cameron believes the record shop filled a gap in the scene: "A lot of house shows, for legal reasons they don't like to publicize where it's gonna be. We're more above ground; it's a store and we're open every day," Cameron explains. "People who don't go to shows very often, don't know what 6th Street Haus is [a punk house in Long Beach], don't know how to get a hold of them, or might not be able to find out about it. And any venue is going to have expectations and want a certain amount of money to be brought in. We don't have any expectations; we're just happy to have the band play 'cause we like the music. If we have no major incidents, we're happy."

Mass Media Records was able to push the record racks normally located in the middle of the store to a back room, but even with this opened up space, when kids started moshing during an Arctic Flowers show, things seemed a bit too chaotic for the small space.

Problems connected to a space being too small will seem minor when one considers that there is total control over that space, which is always a goal for punks hosting shows. But not everyone can be so lucky. Jordan Brand tells me that after the Cog Factory closed he had to bounce around from space to space, often finding a good fit for a few months to a year. Then the new space would come undone for one reason or another and he would have to chase down another location. For example, he worked out a deal with a fraternity to use a garage. But one night some fraternity members and their girlfriends wanted a show to end early so they could watch *Swordfish* on DVD. Then he had to move a show that had been scheduled at a local skatepark. The owner demanded that the skatepark would provide the door person even though Jordan always used a trustworthy friend to work the door after being burned by door guys who let friends in for free or decided to change entry fees without consulting Jordan. This guy at the skatepark tried to change the terms of their deal whereby the first $175 would go the space and then there would be a 50-50 split of the door after that. After the bands all agreed that this was untenable and that the show would be moved to a local house, the guy told Jordan: "You don't understand how shows work" even though Jordan had been booking shows in Omaha for six years. Jordan adds that the overall experience was "a really beautiful thing" because all of the punks and metal kids in the parking lot waiting to see the show started sharing information about how to get to the house, understanding that there were a bunch of suburban kids who weren't regulars at the house where the show would now happen. He says that it was one of his favorite basement shows ever. "It sounds crazy but when you have that big of a group of people that just dealt with that kind of bullshit and we won, there was just this energy that night."

The cooperative bonding that Jordan describes is the kind of ideal that many show promoters hope to foster in their scenes. Unfortunately, every story shared about punks working together to make things happen can be balanced with more negative narratives about punks undermining their own scenes. The last show the Cabbage Collective booked at Calvary Church was Spitboy, Citizen Fish, and Policy of 3. "Folks showed up and were drinking in the bathroom and broke bottles outside. That didn't bode well with neighbors, and the space was essentially a community center." These actions meant the space was no longer available for punk shows.

The whole scene can be let down by the actions of a select few fools. Will Dandy writes in his July/August 1994 column in *Punk Planet* about organizing a show in Alabama for Unwound. He and his friend rented out a community space to host the show, but by the end of the night he was "pissed off at punk rock and punk rockers" after dealing with a series of problems: dividers between urinals were knocked down in the bathroom, a sink in the bathroom was pulled off the wall, and someone broke a window. "These people who were just 'living the chaos' were causing problems for other punks." Will notes that he could see the woman who rented out the space thinking that the punks were trying to break everything they could. He argues that violence and destruction do nothing but harm to the punk scene; the destruction costs bands money and makes it harder for people to organize shows.

The problems intensify when the size of the show increases. A large punk show that might draw some part-time punks is more likely to experience problems than a DIY show, which tends to be attended by punks who are part of a DIY scene.

Changes within a scene are perhaps the number one reason that punk spaces don't last. Bob Suren writes in the March 2011 issue of *Seven Inches to Freedom* that he moved to Brandon, Florida and opened Sound Idea there thinking that a particular group of people would become regulars at the record shop—but that never happened. "And over the years there was plenty of turnover. Some people would be daily fixtures at Sound Idea for six months, a year, maybe two years and then they'd vanish, only to be replaced by a new crowd. Sometimes there were overlaps in the crowds. Usually the 'new' crowd would grate on the nerves of the 'old' crowd and the old crowd would just drift away." Bob writes that this general shift was depressing and he wonders whether the change in regulars was tied to something he did wrong. "But I guess that is the nature of the underground music scene." In some sense, the record-buying punks tend to last longer than the show-going and the show-promoting punks. If Bob was seeing turnover in his shop, he was not alone.

DIY spaces form and shut down too quickly. Some spaces have had a great run, but that longevity is rare. And given the problems discussed previously with landlords, police, and neighbors, the house venue seems to have the shortest lifespan of the various DIY show spaces.

As Chuck Coffey tells me, "It seems that it's about two years before you hit some make or break point where someone's getting on your nerves or you've lost interest musically and want to do something else. And I think the same can be said for venues. Most of these are run by more than one person; it's a collection of people similar to a band and they want to do other things. I'm sure that what happens is that just as bands break up, as a group of people they want to go somewhere else or do something different. If you don't get someone to take over the space then that's the end of the space." There is also the reality of burnout. Nicole Pagowsky describes this general feeling to me, saying: "Being so organized, I put so much effort into everything from the flyer design to promoting everywhere and then kind of babysitting people all night. Plus there was standing at the door to take money when people were jerky about it sometimes." All of this workload started to take a toll on her.

I think the longevity of spaces is also directly tied to when houses are formed, given the age of the renters. Punks are willing to live amidst the chaos and dedicate time to punk when they are in their early twenties but after that they're starting to partner off, they have kids, their jobs start to require more time, and they become busy with other social activities. "When you're younger, you don't care as much about what gets messed up in your house. Or if there's always a bunch of people or if it's always dirty," Jenny Ray tells me. "For me, I think it was getting older that made me not want to have a house where I have shows all the time. I don't have a ton of nice stuff, but you start to get nicer things and start to get an idea of how you want to live. I do think it takes a certain person, a person who is going to be open-minded and understand that there's going to be times when there is a whole shitload of people in your house and you don't want them there, but you're doing it for the scene, the community, and for the band to get to the next spot." She adds that the big issue for people in punk houses is deciding if they want to deal with the chaos of living in a show space and then deciding at what point such a life is no longer attractive.

"This has been a theory of mine, although you and I sort of go against this," Dave Zukauskas tells me. "The scene sort of turns itself over about every three years or so. Bands tend to last around three years. People tend to go to shows for around three years. Maybe it has to do with college. People get involved in college when they are freshmen or sophomores and they give it up. Or maybe it has to do with something else." Dave adds that these demographic changes also have regional counterparts in Connecticut, where different parts of the state become hubs for activity but then die off. "At the very beginning it was Fairfield County near New York, where the Anthrax was. Then in the '90s it was stronger in New Haven. A lot of bands in New Haven and a lot of shows because of The Tune Inn. Now there's a lot of shows in Hartford. Back in the '80s you never saw bands or shows in Hartford, or very rarely. As it starts to die out in one part of the state, you give it a year or so and it starts to pick up somewhere else."

In the April 2011 issue of *MRR* Paul Comeau asked Sean Murphy of Whitney House in Hartford about the house's future. "It will die," he replied. "That's how these things go. The pessimist in me tells me that once this ends we'll go back to square one with nothing in the area. The optimist in me says someone will keep something going. I prefer the latter, but it's not my decision to make, it's everyone else's." Whitney House is still going and Sean is still involved, but more than likely his presence has contributed to the longevity.

Punk is both ephemeral and stable. This combination helps shape an interesting and unique music and culture. Turnover itself is not a problem, but the constant flux within punk means that similar mistakes are made that could have been avoided if important learning experiences had been regularly discussed within a scene. "Maybe some of that knowledge is lost along the way," Bull Gervasi tells me. "So there's always going to be new kids coming in and some know better than others what they're doing or how they're doing it. All of the bands I've played in have been touring within that DIY scene circuit and always wanted to try out places we hadn't been to instead of just going to Chicago and playing with our friends there, or Austin, or other kinds of places that have long-standing punk scenes that you don't have to worry about. We knew that if our buddy in this place was doing the show then we wouldn't have to worry about anything. I wouldn't have to bug him about getting flyers out or having a space confirmed. We just set the date and we're done. But if a kid contacted us from some random place in North Carolina that we've never been, or never heard of, and is real psyched to do a show for us then we're gonna try and make that happen. Sometimes it might go better than others."

The opportunity to quickly move from being part of the crowd to becoming more involved is part of a punk's DNA. The problems with such inexperience can be balanced out with the excitement that buttresses a new promoter's efforts. And that passion can be important for punks like Bull who viewed the experience of touring to be so crucial to his individual growth as a person and a politicized punk.

It's important to add, though, that how a scene changes will depend on the ways that different generations of punks interact. Bob Suren described a lack of relations among punks of different generations in his shop and Chris Moore tells me that something similar happened in Washington, DC when he was first going to shows. "I think that me being young had a lot to do with how I felt at the shows. It was a less inclusive environment. At the time I was going to shows and the majority of the people were older and a lot of their bands were breaking up. They were kind of set in their ways and not very welcoming of younger people," says Chris. He claims that things are very different in that scene now. "The older people are super-inclusive of younger people; it's much more inviting. Sure, punk is not for everybody. But who are you to judge what person deserves to be into punk. Everyone starts from somewhere. Tons of young kids are doing shows in DC right now and it's really cool. And those kids are into getting younger kids out."

Punks have a sense of what should happen in a scene and why, but they ideally avoid the punker-than-thou approach to doing DIY that can be prevalent in some spaces. "I wanted everybody to feel welcome. I used to joke that I call it missionary work, where I was trying to convert them to something that was more positive that they got something out of," Jordan Brand tells me. "I used to get a lot of criticism because I would invite some of these kids who were in crap bands. They would bring in a bunch of kids that weren't into the type of music that the touring band was but after they saw them they were like, 'This is great.' Those kids became the people who played the innovative music later and got into cool things. Somebody's gotta help you along the way. Nobody was born with a mohawk."

Jordan and other punks were invested in mentoring through interpersonal relationships. A new media environment facilitates a greater collection of resources, but a move from word-of-mouth to electronic word-of-mouth can lead to less interesting approaches to DIY shows. During the pre-Internet days scenes required a combination of a lot of planning and the ability to be extremely flexible. Touring bands and promoters had to be smart about working well in advance to schedule the best tour options. Saira Huff tells me that Detestation formed in 1995 and quickly started doing regional tours, traveling from Portland down to San Diego or from Portland up to Vancouver, because there were enough places to play in between. A band comes through town, a show is played together, a friendship is formed, and shows are traded. But other tours to the Midwest involved a more complicated foresight. "Our bass player had been in a bunch of other bands and he and I had a record label so people were always writing us about his bands or our bands or Detestation coming out. So we would just save their letters and a lot of times they would send a phone number and we'd call them and they would let us know where would be best to play."

Dan Dittmer explains that this reality was a crucial influence on the ways that word-of-mouth functioned to shape how punks in Rapid City, South Dakota experienced their scene. "So we even did parks and bridges and stuff like that," Dan says to me. "It was a total swarm effect. Everybody was like, 'Ok, 3:00 at the bridge and twenty minutes before the sound guy would go there and plug everything into the outlets that they have out there. We'd set up equipment and two bands would play. They'd make like $50 and they were good. We did some crazy bands, like Hot Water Music, that way. These kids were so young, they had nothing else to do so we'd call a couple people and it would spread like wild fire and before you knew it you'd have 60 people at the park while a band is playing. Everybody had a good time, people would bring some tofu dogs and eat; it was a community."

This level of networking has expanded with the advent of social media and new media outlets. However, it seems that the flexibility that Dan described features less in punk scenes, which is odd given the instantaneous attributes of texting and real-time interactions among punks through social media websites and apps. At the same time, the ability to network on a more national scale increased radically with the rise of the Internet. Alexander Lesher, for example, says to me that without the Internet "I can't imagine how I would do anything." And Joe Milik adds that MySpace was an important resource for booking bands at the Haunted Basement. MySpace allowed for quick and free communication with people from other parts of the country and for the punks booking that house to hear bands that wanted to play the Haunted Basement.

Al Pist describes how shows at his houses tended to happen via a variety of methods. "By that time we had gotten a computer and were on some of the punk chat rooms (AOL chat rooms), but it was mostly contacts we made on tour." As Detestation did, Al's bands would trade shows with bands from other areas. "And friends of bands that we had played with: 'Hey, so and so gave me your number and said you guys book shows in Connecticut.' Things like that. The word gets around. But a lot of it was bands that we knew that we were friends with from around the east coast. They were coming to Connecticut and probably were going to be staying at our house anyway, so we mine as well set up a show."

If new media can help extend connections among punks across vast spaces, these links also come with problems. The proliferation of media has flattened out distinct features of local scenes, facilitating a more homogenous national experience. Saira shares a detailed assessment of how different cities developed unique scenes but how she noticed the novelties changing over time. "It's only been through moving around that I've noticed this. But in Portland I couldn't help but notice that it was so UK influenced. The UK and Portland are really similar. The weather affects the way you dress. Comparing Portland to Minneapolis, in Portland the weather is very mild. You can kind of dress however you want, which means you can be kind of fashionable. You can wear a studded jacket year-round and you're gonna be fine. Same with the UK. So it makes sense that you would be influenced by people who can afford, for whatever reason, to dress the way you do: Portland the UK. Now, it's also kind of similar to Japan and I know there's a lot of weather similarities. People are looking crazy there in the same way that people are looking crazy in Portland. I feel like there's a blend with that. You can do your hair however you want because it's not humid. And it's not cold so you don't have to wear a hat. It's never too cold and never too hot so you can wear that classic UK style."

She explains that she started to notice the links between climate and culture once she moved to Minneapolis and experienced a very different type of aesthetic. "I'm stepping off the plane in the middle of winter in a studded jacket, I'm like, 'What the hell? This is not gonna work.' I notice that all of the punks there have a different style. They're more crust. Everyone had longer hair, dreadlocks, or stuff like that. And comparing that to Scandinavia. On top of that there's the sound of the music too. Portland is much more mild temperature, so it's not so harsh. The music isn't so harsh; it's softer," she says laughing. "And so I moved to Minneapolis and I'm like, 'Wow! These sounds are much more harsh and fast and heavy.' And everybody looks rough.....You have to wear more clothes and you compare that to the weather in Scandinavia. And there's a huge crust scene there. Harsh crust. Super cold weather and the amount of drinking, the way people drank in Scandinavia and the way people drank in Minneapolis was almost identical. I just feel like it's too coincidental to not feel like there's some kind of effects that that has."

Saira claims, though, that over time the unique cultural differences tied to geographic location started to shift. "It becomes so easy to be whatever you want to be identity-wise," she says in reference to punk scenes post-Internet. "They can just click on something else and be into something else. That's pretty much it. I don't see as much effort, grassroots effort, going into the punk scene as I feel like I used to see. It's a lot more of a passing thing now. Maybe I'm just jaded by this city [New York, which is where she lives now] as far as punk goes, but this last tour I did I was kind of like, 'Woah, this is not very interesting.' In these tiny cities, these small cities, that I used to love. The smaller the town, the better it was, as far as I was concerned. This is going to be the biggest mix of weirdos I can imagine. I don't feel like that so much anymore."

Of course, we should read what happens with the Internet as a source of identity formation in a longer historical context.

This content comes to us faster than past sources of information, which does allow punks to quickly change their interests. But that does not mean contemporary punks are the only generation to be exposed to uniform media content. For example, it is ironic that *Book Your Own Fuckin' Life* simultaneously helped unite punks throughout the U.S. while flattening out the punk experience by helping kill off some of the unique localism. Punks learned about types of show spaces in other cities and could attempt to replicate shows in similar spaces in their own cities. The same imitation could happen with record stores or vegan food options, dumpster diving, etc.

Another issue that has been exacerbated by a global communication network, although certainly not exclusive to that network, is a commitment to an economic structure that dates back to the early 1990s. The $5 show existed prior to the publicity of Fugazi's tour politics; however, Fugazi's commitment to the $5 show inspired a framing of this price as a norm by various punks from that time into the present. Such choices sometimes link directly to an awareness of Fugazi's commitment to the $5 show and sometimes the $5 norm has emerged via second or third hand narratives about that price's fairness for a variety of reasons. Prior to the 1990s many shows were actually cheaper than $5, so it's not as if this price has ties to punk's formation. While Fugazi's politics were admirable and their music was exciting, those prices were able to sustain the band on tour and after tours because they were a popular band. They built that reputation over time, smaller bands aren't going to play shows to 2,000 people and earn a large percentage of $10,000. Also, gas is more expensive, food is more expensive, rehearsal spaces are more expensive, and rent is more expensive. How are punks supposed to maintain some sense of balance in their lives when the cost of living has gone up but the cost of a show has mostly stayed the same? Shows that feature multiple touring bands merit donations in the $8-10 range.

I understand that some punks would have a hard time managing that price increase, but promoters usually know who is struggling financially and who can afford the donation. To this end, adopting a sliding scale for all shows would mean that people who can afford more would ideally pay more. I always pay the top end of a sliding scale when that donation structure is used and assume that other punks with steady jobs do the same. Moreover, perhaps a little less (corporate) beer at a BYOB house means a little more money for the bands. As Vic Vicars tells me, "This sounds so cliché I know, but rather than going to bars or to a huge show where there's no connection, that's not what I like about music. Playing in a band, I like meeting people; I like making friends with people who have similar interests. The same thing goes for booking shows. You book bands that you think you will like. You cook them food and you become friends and you stay in touch. It's not this weird rock star kind of thing: 'Hey, get me my blue M&Ms.' We're just men and women who have similar interests and we can connect on a level that I think is really lacking in other places. Even smaller bar shows, when I meet guys it's definitely like, 'Hey, we're a band. Take us seriously because we're a band.' I don't care about that. I play music, yes, but I never consider myself a musician. I like the fact that you can develop a relationship with this person if you wanted to; they're not out of reach." The experiences are crucial for touring bands, local bands, and punks in a local scene, but for those positive encounters to continue we need to support, in the best way we can, people who help shape those experiences.

Punk has a rich history and yet a short lifespan. Punk's longevity is collective, whereas the individual parts that help make up the culture at any given time tend to converge and then come undone rather quickly. Volunteer-run spaces are often created with a plan to buffer against such problems, house shows are tied to this lifecycle in ways that limit the longevity, and other types of DIY spaces might fall somewhere in between. In the end, what matters most to me is a relationship to the music and connections among punks to make a scene. I remain excited by the creative efforts among punks to find spaces to stage shows, which ultimately happens at a local level. The choices that punks make about where to do DIY shows (houses, volunteer-run spaces, the woods, boxing gyms, record stores) often require negotiation with, and sometimes efforts to evade, a variety of mainstream individuals and institutional forces that attempt to limit such underground efforts. In the face of such struggles, the creation of house spaces, volunteer-run spaces, and other punk-specific locations truly materialize DIY in powerful ways that also model what it means and feels like to do DIY together.

Acknowledgements

I want to thank the many punks who were so generous with their time and creative energies as I conducted research for this book. I appreciate their willingness to talk with me about their hopes, frustrations, and general experiences in the scene. Similarly, I am grateful to the photographers who generously agreed to share their work through this book. Such generosity is an extension of what has been happening in a course I teach every autumn for incoming freshmen at DePaul University. During the past ten years multiple generations of Chicago punks have talked with my students about doing DIY punk in Chicago. I learned a lot from those conversations, which is ultimately reflected in this book.

I also want to thank my colleagues in the College of Communication at DePaul University. A DePaul URC research grant helped fund research trips to visit spaces outside Chicago and a College of Communication Summer Research grant freed up time to transcribe interviews. Similarly, I thank my friends and colleagues with whom I have worked closely over the past few years, helping me grow as a teacher, researcher, and writer: Mary Gould, Michael LeVan, Joan Faber McAlister, Mark Neumann, Raechel Tiffe, and Simone Tosoni. A special thanks to David Wellman and Lou Rutigliano who regularly join me for shows in Chicago and offered feedback on my early musings about the reasons why a book about DIY punk spaces could be interesting.

Everyone at Microcosm has been wonderful to work with. I am especially grateful to Joe, Taylor, and Elly for helping guide this project to completion.

Finally, I thank my family members for their continued patience and encouragement. Researching and writing this book was not only a major emotional and temporal commitment for me but for them as well. This is especially true for Melissa and Zoe Makagon. Zoe attended her first house show with me at Mousetrap in April 2015 (Rule of Thirds, Negative Scanner, Daylight Robbery, Torture Love, and Supreme Nothing). I'm hoping that many more will follow.

86 Mentality, Albion House, Chicago, IL, October '06